D1382196

ALSO BY ROBIN NOBLE

North and West:

Exploring the North and West
Highlands and Islands of Scotland

Castles
in the
Mist

The Victorian Transformation
of the Highlands

Robin Noble

Saraband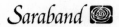

Published by Saraband
Suite 202, 98 Woodlands Road
Glasgow, G3 6HB, Scotland
www.saraband.net

Copyright © Robin Noble 2016

All rights reserved. No part of this publication may be
reproduced, stored in a retrieval system, or transmitted, in any
form or by any means, electronic, mechanical, photocopying,
recording, or otherwise, without first obtaining the written
permission of the copyright owner.

ISBN: 9781910192344
ebook: 9781910192351

Printed in the EU on sustainably sourced paper.

10 9 8 7 6 5 4 3 2 1

For my brother, Rhoderick,
with whom so many memories are shared

ROBIN NOBLE has lived in various locations in the Highlands and Islands since the 1970s, and has worked as an interpreter and teacher of all aspects of the wonderful landscapes of the north of Scotland since joining the Orkney Field and Arts Centre in 1980. Since then he has had roles at Aigas and Kindrogan Field Centres, worked for the universities of Aberdeen, Glasgow Caledonian and Stirling, and lectured in local village societies, clubs and on cruises. He has led countless groups in addition: Caledonian Wildlife, The Travelling Naturalist, The Smithsonian Institution, The Philadelphia Academy of Natural Sciences, Harvard Alumni, and many others. His interests are holistic, including introductory geology, natural history and history. His deepest studies have been of the native woodlands of northern Scotland, and its fascinating archaeology. He continues to work for Aigas Field Centre and the *Hebridean Princess*, as well as working on his own writing and study. *Castles in the Mist* is his second book.

CONTENTS

FOREWORD

I have known Robin Noble for forty-five years — a working lifetime. He was the manager of our little field studies centre at Aigas for some of those years and has remained closely in touch as a consultant and trainer of young staff ever since. Many of the best attributes of our work with the general public visiting the Highlands stemmed from his ideas and enthusiasm, something for which I shall always be most grateful.

Amongst the reasons why Robin's work with us (and indeed his friendship) has endured for so long are his remarkable wealth and breadth of knowledge and his irrepressible enthusiasm for his subject. Robin is very unusual. He is an extraordinary generalist — a naturalist, a historian, an archaeologist, an ornithologist, a woodland expert, a geologist and many other —ists, including whatever sort of an —ist properly understands the significance and formation of soils to just about everything that grows or moves above them. That immediately becomes clear very early in this important little book.

I feel very honoured to have been asked to write this foreword and to appear from time to time in the text. As I read it I found myself with him again, at the fireside, whisky in hand, debating Highland Clearances, or the overgrazing of the hills by deer and sheep, or perhaps just reliving the wonderful sightings of wildlife we have enjoyed together down the years. I do not know anyone else who has such a comprehensive understanding of the Highlands we both love so much.

JOHN LISTER-KAYE
House of Aigas, February 2016

INTRODUCTION

The passing of time alters one's perceptions. Now being over sixty, I perceive with something of a jolt that I was born approximately halfway between the end of the Victorian era and the present day – in fact, a little closer to 1901, when Queen Victoria died, than to 2015 when I am writing this. As a family, we had a considerable interest in the past; my father read History at Cambridge, and my grandmother was a keen amateur historian. Perhaps more significantly, our awareness of the past was heightened by the number of generations with whom family members had been in contact. My mother knew her great-grandmother for many years, for instance, and my eldest daughter was twenty when *her* great-grandmother died.

It would be wrong to suggest that we had any great feelings, as we grew up, for the Victorian era, but there were some reminders of it around us. My Highland grandmother was born in 1896 and had vague memories of the national feeling when Queen Victoria died. We were familiar with photographs of my great-grandfather (her father), who was something of a family hero because of his important work in devising effective fortifications against U-boats in World War I. In his busy retirement, he wrote books and founded the Clan Munro (Association), an initiative that was entirely in keeping with the spirit of the Balmorality epoch.

A portrait of *his* grandfather was hanging above the long flight of stone stairs leading up to our bedrooms. In that painting he was clad, appropriately, in kilt, plaid and tartan hose, with bonnet and crook. He was bearded, and his clear eyes, well-marked eyebrows and thin, high-bridged, aquiline nose – real Highland characteristics – lived on in my grandmother. We later learnt that Queen Victoria had known this face: our portrait was a copy of one of the splendid series of Highlanders painted for the Queen herself by Kenneth MacLeay. Why Donald Munro was chosen to represent his clan in these pictures we never learnt, but we were lucky enough to be permitted to obtain photographs of the original. One hangs in my bedroom today.

We did not have television during my childhood, and we read avidly. I greatly enjoyed the Jacobite novels of D.K. Broster. She was born during the reign of Queen Victoria, and captured wonderfully the romantic aspects of the Highlands and the ill-fated Jacobite Rising of 1745. I think it was in the school library that I first found the works of another author who came to mean a lot to me. Like his fellow-writer and excise-man, the much better remembered and more complex Neil M. Gunn, Maurice Walsh was very much a writer of place, particularly the northern fringes of the Eastern Highlands – the counties of Banff, Moray and Nairn – which was an area famed for its distilleries. As it happened, my father had later trained in Speyside's distilleries and cooperages, and so we got to know precisely the places that featured in Walsh's books. Those novels, now mostly forgotten, were of the 'rattling good yarn' sort, with long walks, climbing, poaching adventures and the occasional good fight. But they always centred around the Highland sporting estate, the defining attribute of Balmorality.

As a young boy I had not been very conscious of the whole sporting culture, but once sent away to boarding school, which I very much disliked, I met other boys whose families were as 'North-oriented' as mine, who either owned, or lived on these sporting estates. (As far as I was concerned, my school, on the damp fringes of the Highlands, was still Victorian in spirit; I had missed the cold baths by a merciful term or two, but the school ethos seemed to revolve around rugby, corporal punishment and the militarism of the Cadet Force.) I began to realise that some of the activities we, as a family, indulged in while in the North for many weeks at a time were part of this traditional, sporting picture.

We all fished, mostly for brown trout, although I was keenest on luring the fighting sea trout from the spate pools in the lovely burn that flowed beside our cottage in Assynt. My father was occasionally given some salmon fishing on the Tay and Isla, catching remarkably few clean fish, but with an impressive average weight of thirty-one pounds. My grandfather was internationally acknowledged as an expert on salmon and salmon fishing, and every year we would head to Loch Stack (dark water backed by the pale and desperate scree-slopes of Arkle) to watch him fish and, we hoped, to go away with some of his catch. None of us did any shooting, although my father stalked the complex Assynt hinterland for some years, and antlers, masquerading as hat-stands, adorned the porch of our family home. Grouse-shooting was way beyond our reach, but every year as we headed north by the road over Struie Hill in Ross-shire, we saw groups of tweed-clad figures carrying guns, followed by dogs, striding over the heather. In later years, much of this moor became conifer plantation, and now part of it, having reached maturity, is being felled; time passes. And I suppose we looked the part, at least at times: tidy clothes were tartans or tweeds. In fact, we were, in some small way, a part of the whole thing.

The years after university saw me working at first in Inverness, then moving back to Assynt for several years before going to Orkney. The influence of the Victorians did not impinge much on office life in the Highland Capital, nor really on my time in crofting Assynt. Nor had I expected to think much about them in Orkney, but there I learnt more about the gaunt Victorian house of Trumland on Rousay. I had known that my grandparents had stayed there, visiting their friend, the archaeologist, whisky-making Laird, Walter Grant from Speyside. My mother had caught her first trout on the Rousay hill-lochs, where I looked for red-throated divers. The photograph survives; my mother, then a skinny tomboy of a girl, clad sensibly but unconventionally in shorts, holding up her catch, standing on the front steps of the big house. I later discovered that same house was built for a man who played his part in the Orcadian version of the most notorious events to disfigure the Victorian era: the Highland Clearances.

The next phase of my working life brought me right up against the Victorians and the sporting estate. I found myself based in a typically over-the-top Victorian house, near Beauly in Inverness-shire. I was working with the conservationist Baronet, Sir John Lister-Kaye, running Aigas Field Centre and we specialised in taking people out into, and explaining, the neighbouring Highland countryside and its wildlife. We depended on maintaining good relations with adjacent proprietors, and I began to get to know some of the families who occupy, all year or part-time, these 'castles in the mist'. Quite early on I was introduced to one of them, Peter Fowler, who owned Glencalvie, scene of some of the most well-known Clearances, and a few years later, he asked me to write a book about this beautiful and largely empty, remote estate in central Ross-shire. The obvious way to write a book about the estate was to walk its rough bounds, and the distances involved were, some days, considerable. I was accordingly very grateful to the Victorian owners who had paid for the construction of miles of well-built stalkers' tracks. Parts of them were indeed disappearing under growing moss and bog, which told me something about our contemporary climate, but the critical lesson was the scale of the investment made by those proprietors.

I also got to know again Dunrobin Castle and the man who, ultimately, cares for the whole vast edifice, has inspired much of the new garden, and will be the next Earl of Sutherland: Alistair Strathnaver. His ancestor, the first Duke of Sutherland, initiated a policy of wholesale improvement and modernisation of their vast estates, but that process included the notorious Sutherland Clearances, under which shadow the family has lived ever since. We took many groups of visitors to the palatial house of Dunrobin – they often met Lord Strathnaver – and we discussed the issues involved in this controversial era, during which the face of the great, now largely empty county of Sutherland was fundamentally changed.

During this period at Aigas, I became aware that many of the visiting public who came to enjoy the Highlands and Islands with us, could quite readily take on board (if not completely comprehend) the great geological age of parts of the Highlands: up to 3,000 million years. They readily looked at the landscape in that light, but they had considerable difficulty in assimilating the notion that so much lying above that ancient bedrock is in fact remarkably recent in origin. Most of it derives from the Victorian period.

The famous Battle of Culloden, which took place in 1746, signalled the end of the Jacobite cause, but it also ushered in a period of great change within the Highlands. That transformation began with those who held the land, how they held it, as well as how it was managed and exploited. That process was given a boost when Queen Victoria and Prince Albert first leased old Balmoral Castle and its surrounding lands and continued the romanticisation of the Highlands, begun by Sir Walter Scott in his remarkably successful novels. The sporting estate became wildly fashionable and the creation and acquisition of salmon rivers, deer forests and grouse moors became a major pastime of the rich (astonishingly, perhaps, it persists, even if in somewhat reduced form, to this day). Queen Victoria died in 1901, but the trends of her reign continued until the outbreak of World War I in 1914. That short spell of 168 years – from Culloden to the 'Great War' – saw the Highlands transformed.

The more precise among you will note that I am rather slap-happy in my use of terms. That period of 168 years is rather longer than the Victorian era, but the Victorians saw the culmination of a process begun earlier, and so I will often use that term loosely, as if the old Queen had lived even longer than she did. And I use the term 'Highlands' to refer often to the Scottish Highlands and Islands. Precision can at times be cumbersome and I hope I will be forgiven if I err on the side of ease of reading.

Castles in the Mist is not a comprehensive, academic treatise; it is far more an introduction to a big topic with wide ramifications. It is based on almost a lifetime's acquaintance with the Highlands of Scotland, extensive reading and debate, much touring around, and far more walking. Much observation and thinking derived from those walks, and included in the text are a few of them. They highlight some relevant points, but also, I hope, serve to celebrate what the whole thing is about: this much-loved landscape.

When I look at my country, however, I am far from complaisant, and included in the text are a number of my current worries; a good number of them stem from the Victorian transformation of the land.

Many of you will find some long-accepted ideas about the landscape and history of the Highlands challenged. For all that the Highlands of Scotland are known around the world, they are frequently misunderstood and, while old myths may be occasionally demolished, new myths seem to arise with rapidity to take their place. One example suffices here: the tartan, that inevitable attribute of the Highlands, featuring both in Victorian pictures and modern tourist postcards, used to be described as ancient, 'the garb of old Gaul', whereas now there are plenty of people who will tell you that no tartans existed before Victoria and Albert arrived in Royal Deeside. Neither of these stories is entirely true. While I will try to reveal some little-heard truths, in the nature of things I will repeat other myths or unsupported-but-favourite stories. This is unfortunate but inevitable; all the inaccuracies are mine, and I apologise for them. This type of book inevitably involves generalisations and, while I strive to be careful in mine, equally inevitably, somewhere there will lurk exceptions to what I have said!

At best, I hope to shed light on a recent and crucial period in Highland history, which not only altered dramatically the nature and society of the Scottish Highlands, but whose legacy still presents us with significant problems.

ROBIN NOBLE
January 2016

One

BEFORE THE VICTORIANS

When I was a boy, I began a love affair that has lasted for fifty years. The reason for its longevity might be that it was rather one-sided, to say the least. The object of my devotion was, and has remained, a mountain – one of the strikingly individual hills of West Sutherland in the northern Highlands of Scotland. Quinag and its western cliffs, gullied and buttressed, formed the majestic backdrop to one of the best views of our cottage in Glenleraig. The most obvious manifestation of my obsession was the regularity with which I took photographs of the massif; it is in reality a range of peaks, arranged in a rather curved Y-shape, and looks totally different from around the points of the compass. I had been given a fine camera by my godfather and the result was a veritable torrent of photographs, often of Quinag, which, when proudly shown, would provoke the response, 'Not that bloody mountain again!' (I always felt my family was a trifle insensitive to my emotional needs.)

Many years later, when sorting these old photos, I came to realise that while the distinctive shape of the beloved mountain itself had not visibly changed during all the years in which I had been taking pictures, the appearance of the rest – particularly of the middle ground – had noticeably altered. The change was quite dramatic and inescapable; our small white cottage, for example, had disappeared from view. The reason for this transformation was entirely natural: it was simply due to the visible growth of regenerating birch and alder.

In much the same way, if we could view a series of pictures of Highland scenery through the centuries, it is not the outline that we would see changing. During the period from 1746 to 1914, the mountains themselves would remain recognisable and reassuringly familiar, give or take one or two high-level tracks. It is the fore- and middle-ground that would noticeably change as we work through the decades. The scope of those changes has been comprehensive and we have, of course, no photographs from 1746 to provide us with the starting point of our series of views through time. Instead we must look for clues within the current landscape (and there are a few) and at the various maps and surveys of the Highlands and Islands undertaken in the latter half of the 18th century.

The fact that these surveys were being done meant, in most cases, that change was in the air, that new ideas had come to the Highlands or, at least, into the minds of their proprietors. A nationwide fervour for agricultural improvement had been working its way up through Britain and, in the more stable years that followed the turmoil of 1745 and '46, Highland proprietors began to investigate the potential of their northern estates. The first step was often to commission a survey of exactly what they possessed. In his book *The Age of the Clans* (Historic Scotland/Birlinn, 2002), Robert Dodgshon refers to surveys carried out by the Commissioners for the Annexed Estates, including an especially detailed one of the remote and marginal estate of Knoydart. He also lists the comprehensive Roy or Military Survey of the Highlands, carried out from 1747, Mathew Stobie's plan of the Macdonald Estate on Skye (1766), one of Deskie, Glen Livet (1761), and there were a number of others.

When I was around fifteen years old, a dear old lady in the nearby township of Nedd presented me with a copy of the Scottish History Society's *John Home's Survey of Assynt* (Edinburgh, 1960), carried out for the Sutherland Estates. John Kirk, a surveyor from Edinburgh, had originally started on the project, but he fell ill and died in the summer of 1773 and work did not restart until the early summer of 1774, when Home, accompanied by two assistants and four lads, took up the task. The landscape of Assynt is in every way a remarkably complex one, intricate and craggy, haphazardly strewn with lochs and lochans of irregular shape, and within this awkward setting Home mapped the settlements (called 'farms' at this time), their infield and the sheiling-grounds (summer grazing areas), along with the farm boundaries. The existing woods also featured, so figures for the areas of the 'Infield, Sheelings, Natural Woods, Hills, Moss and rocky Muirish Pasture and lochs' were all provided – a remarkable achievement, as anyone who knows this wonderful area will agree. By far the largest part of the whole parish was characterised in this evocative phrase: 'rocky Muirish Pasture'. Looking by chance at the figures for the farm of 'Culack', I see the rough totals as follows:

Infield: 52 acres
Sheelings: 16 acres
Natural Woods: 112 acres
Hills, Moss and rocky Muirish Pasture: 1856 acres
Lochs: 4 acres

The phrase 'Hills, Moss and rocky Muirish Pasture' is aptly applied to a very large part of the landscape of Assynt (although Home does note areas of good grass within that description). Give or take the proportion of bare rock (very significant in Assynt, but less in many other Highland and Island areas), it could indeed be taken as an appropriate description of the Highlands as a whole and, among other things, does illustrate the limitations of any agricultural improvement. The Highlands did, and do, largely consist of 'Hills, Moss and rocky Muirish Pasture', and the implications of this had to (and still must be) taken on board by anyone who wished to manage this landscape for any purpose whatever.

Discussion of the evolution of the Highland landscape has been rather muddied by a number of factors and it is as well to tackle them briefly at this point. An important but, I believe, largely unrecognised one, has been the unconscious expectation of some commentators that this northern part of the British Isles should in some way – and particularly in the amount of woodland – resemble that of the lowland part of Britain. In fact, as it largely consists of much older and harder rocks, and has a completely different climate, there is very little reason why it should. Commentators, too, have been regrettably imprecise in their use of terminology, especially when describing the nature of the soils and peats of the Highlands, and how they came to be as they are. Terms like 'devastated', 'degraded', 'run down' or simply 'bad and sour' have all been used and I have to make it clear that in an objective, scientific context, emotive terms have no place. There really is no reason why a Highland peat should resemble an English, brown forest soil, and the fact that it doesn't should not prompt the use of terms with any emotional overtones! The problem arises partly from the failure to employ a vocabulary that adequately describes *why* a soil might change: it could occur as a result of entirely natural processes, or because of grazing animals, or direct human action, and it is important to distinguish between these factors. Here it is absolutely critical to emphasise that the soils of the Highlands would naturally have changed through the millennia, even if the human species had never appeared on the scene. W.H.

Pearsall's *Mountains and Moorlands* (Fontana New Naturalist series, 1968) is the great authority on the matter and should be required reading for anyone who wishes to venture into the environmental history of the Highlands and Islands (and, in fact, significant parts of England and Wales as well). Although his writing may be out of date in some particulars, especially in relation to chronology inferred from radiocarbon data, I believe his general analysis remains authoritative.

It may come as a surprise to some that substantial parts of the Highlands, however they may have looked at the end of the Ice Age, began to take on some of their recognisable characteristics quite soon after. Consider, for instance, the attractive headlands of Wester Ross: they are largely composed of Torridonian Sandstone, a massive sandstone laid down in layers so thick that they are in effect impermeable. Sand erodes from this matrix rock and although it may mix in places with humus, it is almost completely sterile and contributes little to the development of anything that might be described as a fertile soil. What can assist in that process is the presence of shell fragments in the shore sand, derived of course from the seabed. The sandstone was laid down in horizontal layers, and in many places remains thus. Any soil that forms on the surface of this unpromising material does, therefore, quickly tend to waterlog and peat will rapidly appear.

Understanding the formation and nature of peat, and the limitations it places on any subsequent use of anywhere so covered, is crucial to the understanding of the Highlands. It is well known (I almost said 'widely appreciated'!) that the Highlands experience, in general terms, a heavy rainfall. Many places throughout the world are similar, but the Highlands have another quality that differentiates us markedly from much of the rest of the world, and that is our generally low summer temperatures. These imply low rates of evaporation of the rain that does fall so enthusiastically, which means all that water hangs around the soil. Few people who have tramped a soggy moor will doubt this.

The heavy rainfall, then, washes components within the soil down towards the often impermeable rock at its base. In particular, mineral traces are washed down and collect slowly in a solid layer, which has been blessed with the name of the 'iron pan'. (I have sometimes attributed this description to early Victorian scientists, but have absolutely no justification for so doing!) The iron pan often appears – for instance, in roadside cuttings – as a rust-coloured band; in such places you may occasionally see groundwater issuing out above this layer, because the iron pan is impermeable. Without disturbance – such as cutting ditches – the soil above will become water-logged, the normal processes of decay of vegetation in air will not take place and there will instead be a slow build-up of the sodden, compacted remains of, particularly, the mosses that enjoy this very specialised, but rather limited, habitat. This is peat and it covers, to one degree or another, a very large part of the Highlands.

Another critical component of our climate is its windy nature. I think you have to live here to gain a true comprehension of exactly how windy many places are, but most visitors will have some inkling. High winds put many plants, especially trees, under stress, but it is the salt-laden nature of our prevailing westerlies that do the most damage. We should bear in mind, too, that long periods of our past may have been windier than the present and this will have had significant effects in simply shifting woods away from exposed locations. Trees will tend to change shape under the influence of regular gales, growing on the sheltered side (normally the eastern) and dying back on the exposed, but nearly all their seed will be blown in one direction, away from the prevailing wind, and that moves whole woods across the landscape – where it is not so water-logged that it will no longer support trees. Trees will simply not grow in the wet and acid environment of deep peat.

One aspect that earlier commentators may not have fully grasped is the reality of climate change as it has affected us in Britain. I have heard it stated that the 'North East Atlantic' – which is exactly where we are, when you think of it – has experienced some of the most rapid and significant changes of climate the world has ever seen. There have been some rather nice long periods of climatic optimum, as for instance in the New Stone Age (or Neolithic), towards the end of which the splendid monuments like the great tomb of Maeshowe, or the enigmatic stone circles like Stenness, Brodgar and Callanish were erected. But there have also been long periods when it became progressively colder, wetter and windier, as in the subsequent period known as the Bronze Age, when great structures could simply not be afforded: life was too hard.

The main point to make here is that once the iron pan has formed, the soil above has waterlogged and peat begun to appear, nothing, short of an earthquake or modern digger, will destroy that impermeable layer, nothing will transform the peat into brown forest earth. In the warmer periods, the surface of the bogs may dry out, and heather and pine, which can tolerate the acidity, will establish there. However, as soon as another downturn starts, the dried peat will waterlog, the sphagnum mosses grow again, and even the pine will give up the struggle, except on a few drier ridges. The process of peat formation may be checked by an improving climate, but it will not be reversed. The overall tendency in a wet climate is inevitably towards the formation of peat and the 'islanding' of more fertile areas where the drainage is better.

Because of all this, many parts of the Highlands actually began to take on their present appearance long before the

Victorians arrived, although, as we will see in subsequent chapters, they did initiate significant, additional change. Critically, too, we must remember that climatic change, and its effect on the natural vegetation, did not stop then; as the Glencalvie stalkers' tracks, disappearing under moss and bog, reminded me, these changes are still ongoing.

Woodland was, of course, a valued resource and it was, equally obviously, so regarded. There are a few clear indications that those who lived in an area devoid of wood had the right to collect it from places that were more fortunate. But it is obvious that by the time of the surveys mentioned above, woodland, however widespread it may ever have been, had, because of the various factors – entirely natural, wholly human-related, and a combination of both – been reduced to a low proportion of the total land area, and these remnants were duly measured and mapped. Some, mainly confined to cliffs and gorges, must have been almost inaccessible, and often still remain to this day. They should really count as natural woodland, and deserve close study; I am far from sure that we understand the natural dynamic of such places. Others, like genuine islands surrounded by water, or scarp woods surrounded by a sea of peat, may have been modified to a greater or lesser extent by grazing animals, whether domesticated or wild, and are therefore categorised now as 'semi-natural' woodland. They too often survive and must have had their own dynamic until the explosion in red deer numbers (of which much more, later).

And the rest, although mapped as 'woodland', was probably something rather different from the woods we now see in such places. Much of it was what we would now call 'wood pasture' and it must have looked much sparser than many such areas now do. It would have been more open and contained managed trees, whether coppiced or pollarded, which were often very large and of great age. We now call them veteran trees. Many deciduous species coppice or pollard well, and in places like Assynt we may still see managed oak, birch, ash, alder, holly and willows, and there are quite extraordinary single-stemmed, pollarded hazels, which look like nothing else I have ever seen. Often, in areas of wood pasture, the trees were pollarded so that the regrowth would occur beyond the reach of the livestock grazed there in winter, enjoying the relative shelter and finer grasses. These woods were just defined as 'woodland', without the 'pasture', because most wooded areas would have been used in this fashion. How else would you combine agriculture and silviculture in an area of such limited fertility and shelter?

In the Assynt woodlands there were small, clear areas to which Home attached the traditional name of 'sheiling', normally used in reference to areas of summer grazing up on the open hill. These areas within the woodland were sometimes very small and were in fact a detached portion of the infield, used for cultivation, perhaps surrounded by a bank or wooden fence. Most woods that we know about were far from being continuous trees, and many had open areas for grazing, others even had small farms within their boundaries. The Black Wood of Rannoch is one such, where you may recognise that you are approaching an old habitation site by the appearance of the trees. Even Scots pine copes quite well with having branches removed, to the extent that some old pines have a profile very similar to that of a pollarded deciduous tree, and these tend to cluster where people once lived and worked the forest. In Strath Farrar, another famous pine wood, a former sheiling site is marked by trees of a very different profile to those on the steeper slopes below.

In some special places, clear evidence remains for what we would now definitely call agro-forestry; the best of which I am aware is at Rassal Ashwood, in Wester Ross. This precious site did not at first appear to be fully understood by its Government guardians, Scottish Natural Heritage (formerly Nature Conservancy and Nature Conservancy Council), and recent actions, unless reversed, will have the unfortunate effect of masking its true nature. It consists of patches of cleared level ground (where crops were grown) and rough, rocky, limestone banks, where hazels and some ashes were clearly managed – especially the hazels. This is one of the best places for seeing the extraordinary single-stemmed, pollarded hazels to which I have already made reference, but unless some grazing is restored to the site, they will continue to shoot from the base, and their amazingly thick and contorted, short trunks will soon rot and disappear.

The name 'sheiling' is generally taken to refer to areas of upland grazing, to which the stock were taken in order to make good use of the summer growth on the hills. Here, the women and children often effectively camped in small huts while tending their animals, milking them and making butter and cheese. The men seem to have commuted between the otherwise abandoned settlements and these places, some of which actually grew hay, emphasising how important the herding of the cattle, sheep and goats must have been, and, most significantly, how limited was the number of deer at this time. Some of these sheilings remain very conspicuous in the landscape, being green and fertile still – they must have shone out like beacons at the height of their use. This system of transhumance to high summer pastures still exists in some European countries, of course, and represents an efficient use of available resources, taking advantage of the hill grazings, while releasing pressure on the areas around the permanent settlements – including, importantly, the woods.

Some of the cropped areas around the permanent settlements are still clearly visible; those at Rassal are level and needed little or no draining, being on limestone, but are clearly indicated by the presence of clearance cairns – small piles of stone collected to one point, allowing the rest of the area to be ploughed. Such clearance cairns, some very large, may now be the only clear evidence for cultivation of former arable areas that have disappeared under regenerating woodland or slowly become bog. In other places, thousands of years of ploughing, or at least centuries, led to the formation of terraces and lynchets.

In places where the soil was very thin, and particularly after a significant increase in the agricultural population around 1800, new arable land was effectively created by bringing up seaweed from the shore, and adding it to manure from the byres and old sooty thatch. This was done in narrow strips misleadingly called 'lazy-beds', and the resulting, corduroy-like pattern remains obvious in many places on the West Coast and in the Islands to this day, despite subsequent flattening by ploughing in some locations. For a long time, areas of arable land had been, like that in the English open-field systems, allocated on an annual basis, but that practice probably died out in different areas at different times and was presumably redundant by the time houses were being built separate from each other, rather than in clusters.

In all these places, a limited number of crops was grown: hay, oats, a type of barley called bere, then subsequently, and crucially, potatoes. Small, walled enclosures, often perhaps later, protected the vegetable gardens or kailyards. Their animals were goats, small sheep and cattle, with tough ponies for the hardest tasks. During the first half of the 18th century, there was a movement towards a money economy, rather than rents being paid in kind, and even remoter, coastal farms in Assynt contributed some cattle to the great droves that began to head southwards to the Lowland markets.

The sheiling huts that sheltered folk in the summer months were mostly cellular in plan, roughly two circles of differing diameters, the larger one being where people slept, and the smaller where the milk, butter and cheese were stored. The use of the sheilings may have begun long ago in the climatic downturn of the Bronze Age, when increasing cold, wind and rain caused the abandonment of the higher ground for permanent settlement and cultivation, while summer occupation remained possible in some places. A number of the huts, such as in Skye, sit on top of substantial mounds, clearly suggesting long-term use of the site.

In some contrast, the permanent homes of the population were single-storey longhouses, originally probably with rounded gables — stronger when you are building without mortar — although later some adopted square gables with chimneys. Some houses are found with both. In Skye, these old 'black-houses' (a name given to them retrospectively, in comparison with later, harled houses) often seemed to cluster in close groups, but in Assynt there is little or no evidence for this settlement pattern, and the houses in Glenleraig, which Home mapped, were separate from each other, scattered along the shoulder of the glen. They may still be seen there, placed (to our eyes) rather randomly along the single-track road, reduced to ruins, disappearing under rushes and bracken, but still reasonably visible.

As structures, such houses are not particularly impressive, perhaps, and it has been customary for many years to suggest that the lives of their inhabitants were particularly squalid and miserable. Like so many Highland stories, there must have been some truth in it, but when one house was excavated (as part of a recent community archaeology project undertaken by Historic Assynt and AOC Archaeology) it turned out to have a sophisticated ducting system regulating the flue in the gable chimney, and it seemed, from the finds made, that the inhabitants had possessed some nice china (Staffordshire Creamware) and had had claret bottles (whether or not they had drunk the original contents cannot really be proved archaeologically, of course). Wondering whether this might be exceptional, given the rather ordinary appearance and context of the house, the team returned to the site in a subsequent year and excavated another, with the same results. There is quite a scatter of structures along this populated side of the glen. In 1775, Home recorded a total of eighteen households, and the population was ninety; this included eighteen folk listed as servants.

Because so much of the popular history of the Highland clans is dominated by cattle-stealing, abductions and occasional atrocious bloodshed, it is often conjectured that the higher echelons of Highland society always resided in castles – no doubt, draughty, cramped and unsophisticated castles, but castles nonetheless. In Assynt, the narrow tower-house of Ardvreck, guarding its headland on Loch Assynt, looks the part. In fact, its early history does seem to have been fairly bloody, but around 1590 it appears that it was enlarged with 'gardens, houses and orchards'. Raiding, however, and various upheavals in the subsequent century saw the MacLeods of Assynt replaced by MacKenzies of Seaforth, Ardvreck Castle abandoned and a new mansion built nearby, close to the present main road to Lochinver. Although it looks as gaunt now as its predecessor, it was described in 1832 as having been a 'Commodious and Comfortable Dwellinghouse', again with a garden attached. For a house built in this northern location and completed as early as 1728, with its fourteen bedchambers, each of which was said to have its own fireplace, Calda House certainly presents an indication of the degree of comfort and simple elegance that was now expected by the Highland upper classes.

But, again unexpectedly perhaps, close to Calda House, up on the limestone ridge above the mansion, are the remains of what might, possibly, be described as the one of the dwellings of the 'upper middle-classes' of the period. The tacksmen, or principal tenants, were sometimes close relations of the landowners and also liked to be housed in some comfort and dignity. The ruins of Eadar a' Chalda are adequate testament to that. Its walls were mortared and around it are several outbuildings, including a byre and two barns. These plain but dignified buildings are often wrongly categorised as Lairds' Houses and are to be found all over the Highlands. Other quite distinguished houses of roughly the same period are located at nearby Achmore, Stronchrubie and Ledbeg. It is a remarkable collection of buildings for what is now a significantly depopulated part of a remote northern parish.

Calda House is distinguished by its double, or 'M' gables, a feature followed in the big houses of Wester Ross (again MacKenzie territory), such as Flowerdale House, near Gairloch, and Applecross, both from around 1738. But there are many other plainer examples, which still give an impression of comfort and dignity in their elegant proportions. Some may go back to the 1600s, perhaps even earlier in Orkney and Skye and East Sutherland, and among the most attractive are Dundonnell in Wester Ross, Ord House in Sleat of Skye, Auchindoune (the Dower House of the Cawdor Estate), and many others. Both Dundonnell and the area around Cawdor possess magnificent exotic trees, some of which must be of significant age and indicate the 'civilised' inclinations of their owners, while the large barns at Flowerdale and Kerrysdale, for instance, suggest the prosperity that permitted such projects. However unequal the division of riches might have been – and there is nothing unusual in such inequality at any time in history (or now) – some folk were clearly prospering.

Two

A WALK IN GLENLERAIG

The cottage that I rent, and which I photographed so much as a teenager, lies on the floor of the long, wooded glen, beside the dark burn. It must have been built some years after 1812, when the township of old houses along the hillside above, was 'cleared', the ninety-or-so inhabitants evicted and replaced by one shepherd, presumably with his family, perhaps with a 'boy' or servant. The building was subsequently added to, then its windows enlarged (mercifully) and a wood-and-corrugated-iron extension later provided a separate bathroom and kitchenette. The solid fuel stove in the living room was still the principal cooker, as well as the source of warmth and hot water. Later again, the extension was swept away and the accommodation, now significantly reduced, was reorganised within the old stone walls.

As so often, I emerge from the front and only door, blink in the bright sunshine and turn right along the rough-harled walls to the gable-end. Here there used to hang a gate, but it has long since had no real purpose, and slowly rotted away. It guarded the entrance to the Back Park, bounded on the hill side by an impressive dry-stone dyke, which was contemporary with the cottage. The dyke and the wide, fast-flowing burn enclose some ground that served at times as a holding area for the gathered sheep, or sometimes for a house-cow. In our youth, my brother and I were rather terrorised by Daisy, a large animal who did not much like small boys, nor dogs, and whose diet was more varied than most. She ate the blowing bottoms of the curtains of my parents' bedroom, was credited with once having tried to eat the tyres off a car, and having drunk a can of paint. None of this seemed to affect her adversely, nor did it much worry her owners: 'It must be a deficiency,' remarked Dannie, the shepherd, philosophically.

In those days, the flat ground of the Back Park was a beautiful natural meadow and, like level patches on the hillside above, awash with flowers in the summer and dancing with butterflies. Sadly, by the time I returned there to live in the late 1990s, all that was just a memory, although I still have the photographs to prove it. By that time, the wetter parts of the glen floor were disappearing under rushes, while the drier areas, once scented and brilliant, were a dense forest of bracken that reached over my head, and would require the aid of a machete to forge a way through in high summer. It is now spring, however, and the bracken just beginning to appear, although it grows astonishingly fast. In any case, I keep instead to a narrow way created by the endless passage of red deer, passing on my left a higher level that must once have been a garden; there are old daffodils blooming there now and a young bird cherry, just coming into bloom, is obviously enjoying the fertile soil. Ahead of me, there is a small rise, with a cliff above the burn and the dark of the Holly Pool; there is still holly in the bushes at its base, but the ordered stepping-stones that defined the end of the deeper water, and heightened it, have long since been pushed aside by spate and uncaring human activity. The far bank is now dense with bushes, but it used to be clear, and this was one of the favoured stances for fishing. I once caught the perfect brown trout here – deep in shape, well-fed and fat, beautifully marked, a lovely creature.

My way dips to where a wooden bridge used to cross the burn; this was the route I always followed as a boy, but the area across the water was subsequently taken over for the construction of a salmon hatchery, and that way up to the Falls had to be abandoned. I continue instead through something of a muddle of regenerating birch and blocked field drains where the butterwort will soon be blooming. A patch of good grass here, beside the swift-flowing water, is rapidly disappearing under great mounds of moss; beyond it, the deer have bashed a hole in the dry-stone wall and here I emerge from the once-cultivated land into a natural tangle of willow, rowan and birch. In places, the walking here is rough, dodging deep mud and slippery tree roots, trying to find stones on which to step, wishing not to fall into the peaty water. Here I once very nearly trod on an otter: both of us deafened by the burn, neither was aware of the other until there was a swirl of dark brown in front of me, a splash, and it was gone. There are hazels beside the water, especially by the next substantial pool, black at the foot of a low cascade and first of the Lower Falls. Again, we mostly fished this from the other side, close to a conspicuously projecting dark rock.

Above the fall, the water flows fast and below me there is a second fall, not so easy to see from this side, but the noise of the water is constant. I used to fish here, too, for the sea trout that would venture upstream after a spate. In my boyhood, I fished constantly (as did my father, mostly on the many lochs), but this struggle to catch a sea trout in the dark pool below the roaring falls was my passion. There is no run of sea trout now; it is almost certain that the commercial salmon farming, with its attendant concentrations of the sea louse, a natural parasite, killed them off.

If, instead of following the waterside route, you head off to the left and a little upwards, you soon regret it, as you rapidly find yourself in a jungle of willow, some standing, some fallen, amid sodden ground. You can just make out the faint outlines of lazy-beds, whose drains have all blocked, causing this chaos of treacherous black ooze. Somewhere in the middle of it all, there stands a large, old alder, remarkable for its shape and the columnar nature of its moss-covered trunk. It grows upwards in two stages, mainly because, I am sure, it was cut – pollarded – at two different heights. This is a managed tree, old enough to have been growing when the ninety folk in the houses up the hill were counted by John Home. Where they tended the lazy-beds, and took branches from the tree, is now a chaos of nature, a shambles of wet and growth, where it is hard to imagine that people ever worked.

Returning to walking by the stream, above the falls, you find that the ground levels out, grass under birches, and the water is much quieter. There seem to be faint hints of a track here, too, and the going is rather easier. I enjoy looking around and the many flowers of the primroses are bright in the grass. There are violets, too, and bluebells and the constant calling of the willow-warbler. This is spring and it is lovely. Here in the gold of an autumn day, I once met a badger coming the other way along a faint track. There are many of his kind in the woods around here and they are often seen in the daytime.

Then there comes a pleasant level area, part-island, with more elegant birches; just below the island, after many years of wandering past, I suddenly noticed the stone footings of a bridge, quite clear on my side, far less so on the other. Presumably the bridge was wooden and led over to the more open, heathery ground of what in my youth we always called 'the Hanging Valley'. Red deer were rare then and hard to see, but an evening stroll up the road to a good viewpoint nearly always showed that the small local herd of woodland deer had cautiously emerged to graze on the heather in the evening sun.

A small tributary descends from the eastern bank at this point and in the spring it is always worth the effort of the short, steep climb up beside it: it flows through a small gorge, and on the almost inaccessible lower banks, ungrazed, the wild garlic (or ramsons) grows profusely and its pungent scent fills the air. Much sweeter and less easy to see, the woodruff is another important flower of undisturbed deciduous woodland, and grows alongside. Just a bit further up, in a side 'inlet' of this side stream, there appear a number of holes, openings of various shapes and sizes amid the wet grass and rushes. If you lie down and put your head inside a couple of the holes, you discover that there is a longish, curving stone-walled chamber below you, and you are looking down through a hole in a fine, lintelled roof. This is a 'souterrain', a storage chamber from the Iron Age in all probability, when meat, perhaps, and dairy products would be stored in its cool, damp recesses.

The surrounding land was once all farmland, although from the few vantage points that get you above the trees, you can mostly identify a sea of birch on the slopes that descend to the main river. This is a new woodland, sprung up since the Clearances. Below the trees – nearly all birch, a good pioneer – there remain some fine grasses and you can trace a lynchet above you if you start the next ascent, past the 'Dark Green Pool' (which I named in my youth) and the Upper Falls, whose own pool was then impossible to fish owing to fallen trees. You could now, if you wanted to, and if you edge round to the obvious, if slippery stance, there is more woodruff, accompanied by wood sanicle, on the damp, vertical slope above you. These are flowers of ancient woodland, and just a small distance beyond lies the wreckage of two ancient and managed hazels, finally mangled in a major gale some years ago.

Beyond this, you find, and must cross, a steep bank; at this point it seems to be mostly of earth, but further up it is much more stony. It is significantly steeper on one side than the other, because its purpose was to keep grazing animals out – out of the arable land through which you have just been walking. At this point I always stop for a while; the burn here is very picturesque, narrow, deep, rushing, splashy, between bare rocks and moss-covered trees. I am always looking for the brilliance of the misnamed 'grey' wagtails here, there are all sorts of places where they could nest – perhaps in the low walls ahead of me, gable-end to the deep stream. This is what remains of the Mill of Glenleraig. The mill-lade itself is tricky to follow; likely it was filled in at the time of the Clearances so that it would never be used again. Its walls are still standing, moss and stone in almost equal proportions, and the chamber into which the lade flowed and where it turned the small, horizontal wheel, is quite obvious.

And, as ever, I have to stop and reflect; this glen is now empty – I am, at the time, the only person living in it – and it is quite unproductive, looking to most folk like a long, beautiful, natural wood running down to the sea. But, only a little more than two hundred years ago, the ninety people living in the glen grew enough cereals to require a mill and a miller. John Home records that his name was Roderick MacKenzie and he had four servants in his household. Perhaps his wife insisted on creamware for her table.

After a while, I continue upriver, out of the woodland and into the open – damp, rougher ground, largely – but even so I cross the remains of two dykes, and in one location, later, the bright yellow globeflower will bloom, incredibly exotic in that damp place, indicative of underlying fertility. This area is wider, flatter than the wooded glen below, and must once have been a lake-bed, dammed until the water forced its way past some obstacle and down its current course. The first part of the slower burn is shallow and there are often dippers here, dapper in their apparent black-and-white, bobbing on the stones. And above this, the nature of the burn suddenly changes, winding deep and slow, sluggish and often impenetrably dark around the wide, peat-filled hollow in the hills, the Ruigh Dorcha, the 'dark sheiling'. It has meandered about here for centuries, creating backwaters and one perfect ox-bow 'lake', perhaps more of a pool. This is the scene each year of the most incredible and noisy orgies, as the toads gather from goodness knows how far around, to enjoy their annual bout of mating. Sex is the only thing on their minds, and sometimes the otters and herons take advantage of this over-riding preoccupation.

The sheiling itself lies on the east side of this mysterious zone and is refreshingly green, obviously fertile to this day, although invaded, as ever, by bracken. It is bounded by a wall and contains a number of structures and low foundations, with a few clearance-cairns in addition. One low foundation is thick-walled and roughly circular, just possibly much older than the others, maybe a roundhouse contemporary with the souterrrain. Inserted into a wall is a very much smaller, cellular structure, often called a 'twinning-pen', where a ewe who had lost her own lamb was shut in for a while with an orphan, in the hope that they would bond, that the lamb would feed, and live. When I was young, the sheep were important here. There are none now, and no shepherd.

But it is spring, and the birds are singing from the brilliance of every birch, there are celandines in the grass at my feet. Life is still good. I contemplate, briefly, a dip in one of the slow, quiet stretches of the river, but it is far too early. The water flowing from the great cliffs of Quinag ahead of me will be freezing. Time to head for home.

Three

THE AGE OF
TRANSFORMATION

I have indicated that, in parts of the Highlands at least, and for some of the lairds, the early 1700s seemed fairly prosperous; a prosperity that might have been linked to changes in the economic life of the area, as new southern markets opened up and a monetary economy began to take over. Clan loyalties might still be significant, but the way in which the people of the clans interacted was beginning, slowly, to change. The early Jacobite Risings of 1715 and 1719 seem to have had a limited negative impact on this gradual process, but that of 1745 was significantly more drastic in its effect. One of the reasons for the ultimate failure of Bonnie Prince Charlie's romantic, doomed attempt to regain the throne of Great Britain for his Roman Catholic father, James, may well have been that the benefits of peace and prosperity were at last being felt even in the remoter parts of the Highlands and Islands, such as Assynt, and it was obvious that another attempt to overthrow the Protestant Hanoverian dynasty now ruling, would, at the very least, threaten that prosperity. It did, for many, of course, very much more than that.

Many historians have analysed the Rising of 1745 and the reasons for its ultimate failure in 1746, on the cold field of Drumossie, now more often called Culloden. It was a war at once civil and religious, so as tangled, nasty and stupid as is humanly possible. But what strikes me most forcibly is that it was a war out-of-step with the times, a throwback to bold gestures and noisy quarrels of past centuries. Old-fashioned honour and loyalty may have brought out supporters like Cameron of Lochiel, but a new financial logic must have kept many at home. Inevitably, the '45 turned back the economic clock for many and reversed the tide of prosperity in episodes of bloodshed, destruction and horror.

There seems little doubt that the Hanoverians did actually, at one stage, feel this was a conflict that they would lose, and George II is said to have been ready to flee from London. His son, the Duke of Cumberland, does not look like a man who showed much emotion, but even he may have had that fear and, efficient and ruthless soldier that he was, determined that he would never feel it again. He then earned his nickname of Butcher Cumberland, both in the way he dealt with captive Jacobites and the way their clan-lands and populations were treated by his men. Large swathes of the central Highlands, especially, were devastated, and the subsequently appointed Commissioners of the Annexed Estates (popularly known as the Forfeited Estates), were faced with something approaching a desert, out of which they were to make peace – and, if possible, some money. Wars are not cheap, and creating peace out of devastation requires investment.

Initially, the great effort was to ensure that such a thing could never happen again; the Highlands had to be subdued for all time. Breaking their spirit with legislation about traditional dress and other matters was not enough. A great, modern, artillery fortress must be built to dominate the area around Inverness, even then the obvious capital of the Highlands. This took many years, and Fort George is still hugely impressive and worth a visit today. After this, the public investment in the Highlands took more peaceful forms.

Early efforts were made by the Commissioners of the Annexed Estates to encourage industry, like the spinning and weaving of linen. Two such schools and factories were established in Wester Ross (just south of Assynt) at Inverlael, close by the head of Loch Broom, and New Kelso, not far from the head of Loch Carron, the latter dating from around 1753. There was another at Invermoriston on Loch Ness. Subsequent efforts at development included the building of formally planned fishing villages by the British Fisheries Society, again on the Ross-shire west coast, at Ullapool in 1788, and Shieldaig. Close to Ullapool, Isle Martin had already been established in 1775 as a fishing station with its own customs house (the necessary salt was then subject to tax), and on another island, not very far away, that of Tanera Mor, largest of the Summer Isles, a herring station with walled courtyard was established in 1785, only forty years after Bonnie Prince Charlie had raised his standard. All this represents a very significant investment within a very short time.

The social background to this development was, however, far from stable. There was, of course, the carnage of the Rising and its aftermath, which must have decimated the young men of many areas, depriving these places of an adequate labour force and drastically reducing economic activity, to the great detriment of those remaining. That would, naturally, apply mainly to Jacobite areas, but life was far from easy even where the clans had kept out of the fighting or supported the Hanoverians. Being linked to southern markets might have brought a measure of prosperity, at least to some if not to all, but, as most of us nowadays are all too aware, markets are volatile and those who depend on them may well be caught out and need to change their activities. Changing the traditional habits, however, of a scattered rural population with very limited options is neither quick nor easy, especially for that population.

I (like many others) have written earlier on the Highland Clearances and their causes in *North and West* (Scottish Cultural Press, 2003) and have no intention of repeating the arguments there presented, but it must be emphasised that this was a period of great volatility on a number of fronts. There was political upheaval with wars in Europe, creating short-term opportunities, of which landowners tried to take advantage. The problem was that these opportunities imposed different requirements, especially for labour. An increased demand for wool, for instance, led to a move towards sheep husbandry, but required comparatively little labour. As has been seen, the ninety people inhabiting Glenleraig and working the land in the age-old way were replaced by the family of one shepherd. Kelp gathering, on the other hand, feeding the infant chemical industries further south, like soap- and glass-making, was labour-intensive. But it took place on the coasts, which were already somewhat congested, and demand fell away rapidly when the wars ended in 1815.

That the population was growing at this time is known, but the reasons for that growth are perhaps not yet entirely understood; one was certainly an increasing reliance by the ordinary folk on the potato, which at first did well, growing on even the poorer land of the West, seemingly impervious to wet and acidity. The climate, too, was changing and the traditional cereal crops began to fail, which increased the reliance on the potato, and the vulnerability of the population were the potato harvest ever itself also to collapse – which, ultimately, of course, it did, in the famine of the 1840s, after an ominous hint of future problems in the 1830s.

Another part of the changing background was the widespread movement towards agricultural improvement, which had begun in England and swept up through Britain. Wherever it manifested itself, it was hugely disruptive; perhaps you have to read the poetry of John Clare to comprehend the emotional impact of the processes, which included the enclosure of common land, but also effected the complete re-drawing of the map of Lowland Britain, with marshes and ponds drained, rivers straightened, villages destroyed, new farms, fields and roads imposed on the ghost of earlier landscapes. The story of this movement – which subsequently overtook Lowland Scotland, the more fertile of the Western Isles such as Islay, and went on to transform Aberdeenshire, the fertile parts of the Highlands like the Laigh of Moray, the firth lands north of Inverness, East Sutherland and much of Caithness and ultimately the lower ground of the Northern Isles – has hardly been told. Although these agricultural landscapes now look peaceful, the embodiment perhaps of rural tranquility, that appearance was not achieved without its own disruption and destruction, and, no doubt, much emotional stress for the population who had it imposed on them.

Much of this improvement of the Lowlands involved drainage, ploughing, fertilisation and new crops, little of which was particularly relevant to the wilder Highlands and Islands, which was mostly rough pasture of the sort described by John Home. To those who were seeking a 'modern' use for the bulk of the Highlands, and higher rents besides, the sheep appeared like something of a magical solution. Its wool and mutton were in great demand (at least at times, but especially when the nation had soldiers to clothe and feed), it required comparatively little input of labour and appeared to thrive even on the rough and wet grounds of the Highlands and Islands. I use the word 'appeared' as there is something of a paradox here: one thing that Highland sheep nowadays excel at is dying, and they suffer from a number of illnesses like liver fluke and foot rot. Probably what really mattered was the profit they could make for the landlord during a fairly short life.

As a result, the movement that may be said to have truly begun in the Highlands in 1782 when sheep were introduced to Glengarry, gained enormous momentum in the early 1800s with Clearances in many northern areas, a process that slowly began to receive the attention of southern media: by 1845, *The Times* even sent a 'Special Commissioner' to examine the latest story, that of the Glencalvie evictions. It was not always a one-way process: there was some resistance, which was occasionally successful (often merely temporary). Neither did those who leased the newly-created sheep-farms always thrive. But, on the whole, the landlords had their way, to which a great number of empty glens today stand testament.

One result of all this change was that a previously rather static population began to move – or be moved. Remarkably soon after the '45, several thousand able-bodied men went to fight in the Seven Years' War in America (1756–63). Others had already emigrated and were caught up in the fighting. The famous Flora MacDonald, who had played a role in the '45, and her husband Alan, were among the latter; they actually returned to Skye but most did not. Clearances continued relentlessly, as emigration – voluntary or forced – began to appear as the only solution to what was now seen as the 'Problem of the Highlands'. Much of this is, of course, well known.

Despite the undeniable fact that the Highlands were in a state of flux, as described above, there were a few, not-very-obvious pointers to a different future. Curiosity lured travellers northwards surprisingly soon after the havoc of Culloden. Thomas Pennant visited the Highlands in 1769, and later Boswell and Johnson made their famous tour, the account of which was published in 1775, when John Home was laboriously surveying Assynt. The geologist J.R. MacCulloch visited the Hebrides in 1799, and the artist William Daniell made his great journey around the islands and north coast in 1815 and left many valuable illustrations, especially of coastal settlements, as well as landscape features like the Old Man of Hoy in Orkney. John Home was nothing like as good an artist as William Daniell, but he enlivened his plans of farms and their boundaries with little vignettes, which repay study. A man is shown working a cas-chrom, the almost archaic but quite effective foot-plough that was part of the old agriculture, which would soon be swept away; he is wearing the kilt, officially banned at the time, but to return with huge popularity during the next century, and men are fishing in Loch Assynt – with rods. The sport of angling, as opposed to the mass netting of fish in estuary, river or loch, had arrived. And a stag is fleeing through the trees at 'Oldernay'. The advent of the sporting estate was nigh.

FOUR

A WALK IN TORRIDON

Today is the first of July and I am further down the West Coast, in the mountainous district of Torridon. I am staying for a few nights in the modern youth hostel by the shore, and have slept reasonably well as the place is fairly quiet. It seems like a promising morning and I have, rather vaguely, elected to do a fairly long walk into the wonderful land between the sea, here at Loch Torridon and the exquisite Loch Maree (freshwater now, although it must also once have been a long, salty inlet). This will take me northwards between great mountains, but I have no intention of climbing any of them; I am heading instead for a quieter, less-known hill.

At first I must drive a short distance along the north side of this sea loch, calm today in the gentle morning sun. The road is single-track, hugging the shore, dominated by a huge upwards sweep of hill, the western end of the ridge of the awe-inspiring Liathach. After a little while I enter woodland, mostly Scots pine, which can tolerate the acidity of the soil derived from the hard sandstone that makes this land. Although the old road continued along the shore, the present public road has to head uphill and slightly inland.

Below me, the woodland falls away, with many fine trees, still mostly pine. Some of them are splendid, and were probably planted, as this is part of the amenity ground – 'policies', we say in Scotland – of a big house. The old public road along the shore was in part taken over as a private drive, although the builders may well actually have paid for the re-routing of public access to the crofting communities further west.

You do not see much of this establishment from the new, high road, but it must be very fine, with a lovely southern outlook over the loch. When it was advertised for sale fairly recently, the brochure showed particulars of a quite restrained and elegant house, with sweeping lawns and big trees; it has four reception rooms, study, gunroom, kitchen, service quarters, billiard room, master bedroom suite and seventeen other bedrooms. You might not immediately realise from such a description that this was built simply as a holiday home, never intended for all-year occupation and probably only used from August till October.

It is, in fact, a typical Victorian sporting lodge and its estate apparently once extended to 17,000 acres, including most of the mountains towards which I shall be heading. I park the car close to the fine river that flows fast and noisily through its dark sandstone rocks, and take the path that I remember quite well from a similar jaunt last year. Summer seems to be coming early this year: the bell-heather is already beginning to bloom; the bright yellow tormentil stars the moss and rough grasses; the heath-spotted orchids are appearing in the damp areas (it is mostly damp underfoot). This is the Scotland – or, at least, the Highlands – of the calendar, or the shortbread tin; the typical image purveyed by the tourist board and, actually, it is good. I am feeling fit and walk briskly, heading for the pass, or *bealach*, that leads between the great mountains in front of me, the peaks of Beinn Alligin and Beinn Dearg.

I have in fact climbed Alligin – many, many years ago – but it was one of those great days that remain in the memory till the end of life, or so I hope. There were three of us, little more than boys, friends from that boarding school on the southern edge of the Highlands, and it was a glorious winter day, with crisp snow, blazing sun and wonderful views.

Today is, by now, promising to be almost as fine and much warmer, so I hasten on, reaching the high point of the *bealach* in an hour. This is quintessentially Torridon, rough going, great lumps of purple rock all round. Beyond this are small lochs, edged with delicate pink beaches and from all sides I hear the plaintive piping of the common sandpipers and watch the flickering of small, tapering wings. Ahead of me are two sizeable lochs, leading northwards, and on the east of each, a long ridge. I am actually aiming for the farthest of these and so must cross the tail-end of a low ridge before reaching Loch na h-Oidhche, the loch of the night; here a single grouse calls. I make a stop at Poca Buidhe. This is a remote bothy, which Niall, one of the boys with whom I had climbed Alligin, and I had visited during a school trip to Torridon one Easter. It was billed as 'Arduous Training', but gave us a one or two good days, of which this was by far the best.

After peacefully eating the first instalment of my sandwiches, I set off along the loch shore, but begin to climb higher quite soon, partly in order to avoid a noisy fishing party who had used an ATV to get to the loch. I am feeling very scornful and puff my way uphill. This is the side of the end of a long hill called Beinn an Eoin, a rather anonymous Highland name: it means 'hill of the birds', normally big birds – in other words, eagles. I eventually reach the northern end of the ridge and then turn to look south along it; this is where I am heading, this is what I have come for, and I seem to have the place to myself. As I stand there, a ring ouzel, a mountain blackbird with a white collar, slips unobtrusively over the short, mossy turf.

By now, it is very bright and I am very hot; shorts and T-shirt go into the rucksack and I head south without a care in the world. The walking is fairly easy, even the 'tower' and 'airy ridge' of which I have read do not worry me, and a golden eagle (slightly tatty, it is true, but a golden eagle nonetheless, and the views of it are glorious) leads me all the way to the southern end of the hill. It pays no attention to the pair of ptarmigan that take off, white wings and grey bodies against the hazy purple-brown of the low ground, to which I must now descend. This looks, and turns out to be, very steep, but it is dry underfoot and I have the time to go slowly down. It does seem a long way and, one after the other, my knees start to hurt. It is many, many years since Niall and I were down there at Poca Buidhe, and I have done a lot of descents in the intervening decades! Eventually, the worst is over and I find myself among some characteristic wet-flushes, where minerals emerge around springs, and the short turf is vivid green. Here I find the lovely starry saxifrage, of which my father is so fond – he and I found it by another such spring high on Quinag one year, again a long time ago. There is also a brilliant, tiny veronica and a willowherb, which I will have to look up when I get back to base – still a considerable distance away.

The next bit of walking is mercifully easier, on huge great pavement-slabs of sandstone, and I begin to recover somewhat and even speed up towards Loch na Cabhaig and the commanding heights of Beinn Dearg beyond, which I must pass before I can enter the *bealach*. Here there are the sad but musical calls of golden plover and, for once, I see them clearly and am able to enjoy the complex, mottled black-and-gold beauty of their plumage, which can be such effective camouflage among the high rocks. And there is churring, too, the call of the little, black-bellied dunlin. Both waders are feeding and breeding in the moorland pools.

Ever slower, now, I enter the *bealach*, but enjoy again the call of the sandpipers and, once emerged into the deep glen between the higher hills, I idle briefly on an idyllic alp in the evening sun. Some way off, I see a herd of red deer grazing quietly, the first of the day, although I have walked silently and kept alert to any signs of them. This is a group of hinds with some calves; at this time the stags will still be living their separate, bachelor existence. And so down the riverside path and quickly into the car, before the midges, enjoying the humid shelter of the trees, decide to attack me.

Later that night in the hostel, dozy after a shower and supper, I recall that Niall and I had been walking in that area with an old keeper (although he was probably only about my current age) as part of a deer-counting exercise. I remember a very nice retired Major (Major Hunter, says my memory out-of-the-blue, but that could well be wrong) explaining to our school party that this was one of – perhaps, in fact, the first – voluntary deer management schemes in the Highlands, with local private estates, the National Trust for Scotland (proprietors of a large part of Glen Torridon) and the Nature Conservancy Council (which owned the National Nature Reserve of Beinn Eighe) all participating. I fear that I was perhaps less interested than I should have been in the ecological significance of this, and more in the possibility of a good walk in the magnificent landscape. We were very lucky with the day itself, which was, for Easter, absolutely lovely and reasonably warm – some of the rest of the week was pretty grim, and the bothy we stayed in of the most basic kind. There was no glass in the windows and I slept deep in my sleeping bag, fully dressed, on a concrete floor, with my head partly under a sink. Despite the late-night larking of a group of lively German boys, this memory makes my night in the hostel seem rather luxurious and I feel content after another good, long day in the hills.

Five

HOW IT ALL STARTED

The next and crucial part of this story is reasonably clear and, paradoxically, remarkably hard to comprehend. Somehow, two writers and a queen (along with her consort prince) inspired a social movement that transformed the face of the Highlands and Islands forever.

The two writers were James MacPherson and Walter Scott. They were both astonishingly successful and influential, which is difficult for us to understand nowadays, given that we rarely open their books. They appealed to the essentially romantic aspirations of a British population perhaps beginning to recoil from the 'satanic mills' of the Industrial Revolution, and inspired a visit to Scotland by George IV, tastefully encased in tartan (until quite recently banned) for the occasion. The fact that George had been much mocked and unpopular in the past appeared to have been forgotten, the climate of Scotland seemed suddenly quite acceptable; the costumes of its inhabitants, once barbaric and indecent, were now noble, fit for a king, and subsequently for a queen and all her family and retainers. Suddenly there was a huge demand for Highland estates and the sporting opportunities they offer; and this has lasted (just, it is true, but it has) through wars, recessions and socialist governments to this day. Why?

It presumably can only adequately be explained by saying that a combination of factors turned out to have huge potency in the minds of the leisured classes of Britain. As outlined earlier, information about the north of Scotland, in journal form at least, had begun to be relayed to the rest of Britain surprisingly early after the '45. The glamorous figures of Flora MacDonald and 'Colonel Anne' (or Lady Mackintosh), both Jacobite-sympathisers imprisoned for a while in London, excited admiration and probably initiated the romance that would build around the ill-fated Rising and its young leader, who escaped to Europe before age and frustration could rob him of his attraction.

James MacPherson appeared on the literary scene and out of the Celtic mists shortly after, in 1760, predating and perhaps inspiring the Romantic poets and Walter Scott, with a huge following across Europe. Scott himself appeared in print with his own poetry, *The Lay of the Last Minstrel*, in 1805, and his first novel, *Waverley* (a story of the Jacobite Rising), in 1814, again building an enormous reputation. He inspired and choreographed George IV's extraordinary visit to Edinburgh in 1821; during the latter's chequered career his rapturous reception on this occasion may well have lingered in his memory.

One of the most dominant themes of Scott's pageantry was the proud re-establishment of the traditional dress of the Highlands and the patterned material of which it was made: the tartan. Although the dress of George's noble courtiers was hardly exactly dull or workmanlike, the tartan, especially perhaps for men, possessed – and retains – an irresistible glamour of its own. Men, it seems, like dressing up, given the chance, and many feel that they look good in tartan. Accordingly, a connection – almost any connection – with Scotland began to seem desirable, especially if it permitted one to wear tartan.

Sporting activity had long been a favoured pastime of

monarchs and the upper classes and so, as the agricultural improvement and industrialisation of southern Britain began to limit the space for such activities, wild northern acres, in general untouched by such developments, began to look attractive. And when sheep farmers began to find it hard to make money, some of the landowners discovered that sportsmen would pay well to stalk the deer that would move on to the ground if the sheep left. That southern Britain was awash with cash, presumably mostly derived from industry, is made clear by the ultimate, if extraordinary, expansion of the sporting estate over much of the Highlands.

Scottish Natural Heritage, the arm of government that took over responsibility for the natural environment in Scotland in 1992, published, quite early on, some 'Occasional Papers' on a number of topics. The two in which I am most interested here (and to which I will return in a later, crucial chapter) were both provided with attractive, eye-catching covers. The first (of them all), in 1993, was entitled 'The Highlands and the Roots of Green Consciousness, 1750–1990' and was written by Professor T.C. Smout, Scotland's Historiographer Royal and, at the time, Deputy Chairman of SNH. The other paper, published in 1994, was 'Ill Fares the Land: A Sustainable Land Ethic for the Sporting Estates of the Highlands and Islands of Scotland', by the then Chairman of the North Areas Board of SNH, John Lister-Kaye, with whom I had worked at Aigas Field Centre. Between them, they build up a picture of the growth of the Highland sporting estate from the six deer forests 'in which red deer were actively preserved for sport' in 1811 (as I have already hinted, deer needed preserving while the human population was increasing towards its maximum in 1846). By 1912, there were over one hundred such forests, and no fewer than '3.6 million acres were exclusively dedicated to deer'. This is an extraordinary escalation from any point of view.

In passing, it may be worth pointing out that the term 'deer forest' never carried with it any implications about the presence of actual woodland. The term 'forest' has nothing to do with trees at all. It indicates an area with particular regulations set aside for the hunting of deer. It is true that some deer forests, such as the New Forest, developed some woodland as agriculture was, initially at least, strictly forbidden. Descriptions such as that of the island of Rum as the 'kingdom of the high (or wild) forest' have been, regrettably, frequently misunderstood and have led to rather too much ecological myth-making.

In the astonishing progression of the deer forest in that short interval of 101 years, it appears that yet more writers may have been implicated in the growth of the cult (a word used, incidentally, in this context by Gavin Maxwell, whose own more recent writings were not without significant impact). William Scrope published *The Art of Deer Stalking* in 1838, the year after Queen Victoria's accession, and Charles St John, an English naturalist and sportsman who lived around the Highlands, published from 1848 a series of illustrated books, which also had a significant following. The extent to which quite remote locations in the Highlands and Islands became fashionable destinations may be revealed in consideration of what had become known as Fingal's Cave on the fairly inaccessible, unpopulated, small island of Staffa. Mendelssohn visited in 1829, and his overture, *The Hebrides*, may have encouraged Turner, the artist (who also painted Loch Coruisk in Skye), a few years later. The poets Wordsworth, Keats and Tennyson went there, as did Jules Verne; and, almost inevitably, Queen Victoria. The process was truly underway.

Victoria and Albert visited a number of Highland locations, including Blair Atholl, Ardverikie on Loch Laggan, and Loch Maree in Wester Ross, before settling on Deeside in what, I think it may fairly be said, became their spiritual home. They made some additions to Old Balmoral Castle before deciding to build a new one, where in future years they would happily spend the months of late summer and early autumn. The castle was ready for occupation by 1855, by which time the prestige of possessing a sporting estate in the Highlands was irrevocably established.

The sporting itself was the critical part of the whole annual performance, and it centred around the deer, the grouse and the salmon, as is well known. Deer had long been considered a noble quarry, worthy of kings and queens, and as the largest wild animal, its status is not surprising. The salmon, too, was perceived as noble, as it leapt peaty falls on its way up the wild Highland rivers, and the fight it would put up if hooked was part of its glamour. The attraction of the grouse was perhaps that there were in fact quite a lot of them around on the widespread heather moors, that their fast flying made them a difficult target, and that young birds, in particular, were (and are) considered delicious. These, and other species, were to be found in a landscape that had come into fashion, and instead of being considered barbaric and ugly, the mountains were fine and wild, and the air pure. This last, to those who knew industrial Britain and its cities, may have had much more meaning than it does now to us. What does have to be recognised is the way in which all these people coped (and many still do!) with the worst of the Highland weather. Queen Victoria seemed impervious to rain and loved the outdoors in all conditions. She would certainly have approved of the late Queen Mother, whose attitude is always said to have been similarly tough.

And then there were the people, the Highlanders, whom Victoria, I think, quite genuinely came to admire and adore. It cannot just have been the tartans or the beards, the music or the language, that attracted her. Nor do I get the feeling that it was all just seen as a picturesque background to her and the growing royal family. Those clansmen she commissioned MacLeay to paint had a mental, almost a spiritual significance to her, and of course, once Albert had died, such folk came to protect her from the intrusions of the complex outside world.

This, however, raises a significant (if rather tangential) irony: one of timing. Only a decade before the new castle of Balmoral was ready for occupation, *The Times* had reported on the evictions in Glencalvie. It referred to 'These poor Highlanders' who, 'apart from their naturally mild and passive nature', had 'been broken in spirit by many such scenes'. That the Queen was quite unaware of the Highland Clearances seems unlikely; what she thought of them, I have no idea. They continued – some in order to allow landowners to create or enlarge sporting estates – until the Napier Commission was set up in 1884, leading, ultimately, to the Crofting Acts of 1886. The fate that was to overtake the population of the Highlands and Islands during the 1800s remains deeply paradoxical; many were shipped away from their native land like cattle, while the more fortunate became trusted retainers to a new breed of landowners.

I was recently discussing this remarkable proliferation of the sporting estate across so much of the Highlands and Islands, and the motives behind it, with John Lister-Kaye, sitting comfortably and most appropriately in his home, the House of Aigas. We agreed that the royal enthusiasm for the entire way of life was crucial, but he emphasised also another element that played a critical part and which we now might easily forget: the aggressive snobbery of the period. 'The rewards of the Industrial Revolution had produced a whole new class of wealthy men desperate to be seen on a par with traditional aristocracy,' he said. 'Having a deer forest was one of the few ways in which the boundaries between new money and old could be blurred.' Snobbery, then, played a role in altering the face of the country – a strange thought.

Six

A WALK IN SKYE

During the long winter nights, one of my favourite amuse-
ments is to read a map, slowly and deliberately, looking at land-
forms and place names, seeking out interesting places to visit.
During the past winter I found one location that intrigued me
very much, and no one I have asked has ever been there, which
makes it all the more alluring.

It has been cold lately; winter this year did not seem to arrive
properly until well into March, when we had brief, but violent
snow showers. Since then it has been very changeable: one day
mild, the next cold, and a few later that were simply sodden.
Then at the end of the month, it became dry and cold, with
easterly winds, which have lately gone round to the north.

By the third of April, I am in desperate need of a walk and I
decide that this same alluring place, being somewhat sheltered
from the coldest winds, is due a visit. Accordingly, I set off
briskly in the car, up the Sleat road to Broadford, then up the
main road as far as Sligachan where I see, to my faint surprise,
that the great Black Cuillin hills are clear (and dusted with
snow, which was more predictable). My road goes west from
here, through a low, gentle glen to the inlets of the western
side, where I turn to the southwest. It seems a long way round,
would almost have been faster by sea (if I had a boat!), but at
last I get there.

I am afraid that I do not find this, my immediate destination, very inspiring. I am at the head of Loch Eynort, one of the sea lochs in this vaguely-named area of Minginish, and the beach is littered, like so many, with rubbish of all sorts – mostly plastic, and very slow to decompose. Ahead of me, the south-eastern shore was once cursed with some truly dismal forestry, much of which has since been felled, leaving its own devastation. The peaks of the majestic Cuillin are visible above this mess, whose steep slopes presumably once had dense birch and hazel; I hope they may one day be replanted with something similar.

At first, too, I am uncertain of my route. I know that I need to reach the skyline ahead of me, above the scattered buildings and old fields, but it is not a way much frequented and I dislike the thought that I may stray into someone's jealously guarded croft. Eventually, I seem to find the right path and reach the Bealach na Croiche, a low pass through to the real objective for the day. I am not entirely sure of the meaning of this name, and am reluctant to consider it for too long. *Bealach* is the word for 'pass' or 'col', but *croiche* or *croich* may mean 'gibbet' or 'gallows', which I would rather not think about, and in any case, hardly credit – who would ever build a gallows here? At least the view is good.

Ahead of me is a broad, open, gentle glen; it is quite short, running from a high, sheltering plateau to the north, and with protective ridges on the western side and on the eastern side, where I am at present. It is, therefore, south-facing, looking to the sun, the further coast and, depending exactly where you are, the group of the Small Isles. It is grassy, with hardly a bush, and a rusty staining on the green that indicates the presence of much bracken in summer. And I can see already, because much of it lies before me, that it boasts an extraordinary extent of lazy-beds. No one lives here at all now, despite its attractions, but many did at one stage. There are a number of buildings visible to me, all roofless, numerous lower foundations of flimsier structures, and dykes, presumably the usual part-turf, part-stone mixture, going in different directions. There are lots of sheep.

A burn runs through the wide glen, and I decide that I will first follow it towards the sea. It is remarkably easy walking on the short grass, being dampish, just a bit slippery in places, and a few sheep scatter in exaggerated alarm at my brisk approach. One or two, I note, are dead, little surprise after a hard winter, and two golden eagles lift effortlessly into the air from one of the carcasses.

After a little while, I reach a couple of prominent stones, short, almost perfect columns of basalt (all of Skye north of the Cuillins is volcanic in origin), some distance apart. I am surprised, and surprisingly moved, to see that each has a simple, incised cross on one face. Between the stones and slightly above is a bluff (a flat-topped bank), and I decide that I must be 'meant' to climb up on to it, which I do. There are foundations up there and I am sure there are traces of a rectangular structure within a surrounding wall. The logical deduction seems to be that I have discovered the site of an early Christian chapel, marked by contemporary, simple crosses. This is exciting and I resolve to check this out later; the map certainly shows no such remains.

I spend a while longer here, vaguely pondering and photographing, before continuing to follow the burn. A fine waterfall, looking rather Icelandic as it cascades over the volcanic escarpment, makes an excellent place for my first sandwiches, and I realise that the community of this particular glen, unlike most in Skye, had no easy access to the sea – it is blocked by steep rocks and abrupt cliffs. The inability to beach-comb, to bring a boat in, to harvest seaweed, must be the first negative aspect of this beautiful glen. The gentle April sunshine is most welcome, warmish, and I am becoming very fond already of this place, which I have discovered for myself.

From here, my way lies westward and involves something more like climbing; the scenery becomes steeper, more dramatic, as I head up by the gorge of Caladale and past Ben Scaalen, where I have excellent views of a sea eagle, bigger, broader, more vulturine than its golden cousin, and it flaps heavily, as if those huge, wide wings are a real burden. All over this area of Skye there tend, at least some years, to be rabbits in plenty for the eagles to feed on and if not, there is always, somewhere, a dead sheep. They are good at dying.

I am now heading north, with the abrupt, basalt-column-sided hill of Preshal Beag in front of me, but I have not the time to head into that equally glorious country; besides, it is best approached from Talisker (which I must do again soon). On this occasion I must keep ascending, on to the peaty plateau of Beinn Bhreac. I keep close to the edge of the plateau, partly because the views down over my wide glen are splendid. Suddenly there is another eagle, close to me, gliding infinitely slowly, without flapping, into the gentle, if cold, wind – they really are the masters of the air, and the afternoon sun emphasises the golden nape of this majestic bird.

I stop eventually on the edge of the escarpment, investigating a small, abrupt, cliffed eminence. I believe that I can trace the remains of a stone wall around it: once, long ago in the Iron Age, it must have served as a very windy but strong refuge and lookout. Below is the smooth, fertile glen into which I must now descend. It is, again, extremely steep and I have sore knees long before I reach the more level ground.

Here, though, I am intrigued by more substantial ruins: there is a house, surrounded by lesser structures. Its walls are mortared, their volcanic stones big and dark; even in ruins it retains dignity, and has a beautiful outlook. For some reason, I am impressed by it and have a sense of significant antiquity. I want it to be older than simply a tacksman's house of the 18th century. It reminds me somewhat of the slightly larger, similar house with a strange bowed end on Rudh' an Dunain, not that far away, and said to be the residence of a minor chief. I want this to be the same kind of thing; is it simply a romantic stirring, or an instinct awakening after viewing many such old houses?

Full of delight, I follow the burn back down, hearing golden plover and seeing the first wheatear of the year – a typical place for them, they actually like sheep or, at least, the flies that cluster around their droppings (lose the sheep, and within ten years you will lose the wheatear). I revisit the chapel and then the waterfall, and then have a very quick, freezing dip in the superb pool beneath.

Enlivened by this, and fully aware that evening is approaching and the day cooling down, I make a brisk re-ascent to the *bealach* that leads me down again to Loch Eynort and my car.

Throughout this account I have not used the name of this wonderful place; it is partly a silly wish to keep its location to myself, which is ridiculous as it can, obviously, be easily found. It is also because I have struggled to find a possible meaning of the name – which is Tusdale. It is certainly Scandinavian – Viking – in part. The 'dale' element crops up throughout Scandinavian Scotland (and northern England) and means 'valley' or 'glen'. The first element defeats me: it looks like nothing I can find in Gaelic, and not much that is relevant in Norse.

It appears to have been a generally prosperous place in which to live, despite its relatively poor access. After the Clearances it certainly became, as it still is, a sheep-run; a walled park, like that behind my cottage in Glenleraig, was created, and the lazy-beds within it, partly levelled by ploughing. The sheer extent of the lazy-beds is remarkable, even in the context of Skye, where they are very noticeable.

Seven

BUILDING THE BIG HOUSES

Soon after the disruption caused by the Rising of 1745, some families began building substantial houses again – often because they had to. It is not exactly clear whether Foulis Castle in Ross-shire, the home of the chiefs of Clan Munro (who had long been strongly Protestant and opposed to the Jacobites), had merely been regularly plundered or actually burnt, but the then new chief, Sir Harry, began to build in the early 1750s. He incorporated some parts, at least, of the old castle in his new venture, completing the tower, which is prominent from the courtyard, by 1754. It appears that he subsequently pulled down more of the old house and further extended the new, embellishing the south front with a pediment containing an armorial panel of 1777, all above an even later grand entrance.

As a piece of architecture, Foulis is particularly harmonious and elegant; reference to the building itself, and its plans, makes it clear that the apparent symmetry was not easy to achieve, and that significant structural risks were taken in reworking the main entrance and creating a new hall and stair. The tower is one of the most original and successful of its type in Scotland, let alone in the Highlands.

For a while it seemed as though the classical elegance of Foulis would become the norm throughout the wider area. A print of Cromarty Castle from 1746 appears to show a great crack running down the tower; it was, in any case, soon swept away and replaced by an imposing and accomplished mansion in a purely classical style, which dates from around 1772. This has some resemblance to the tall, new Culloden House outside Inverness. Bonnie Prince Charlie spent the night before his last, fatal battle in the old house of that name, but it was largely reconstructed in the 1770s. Other significant classical buildings cluster around the Firths: they include the splendid Tarbat House (quite close to Invergordon), Conon House, and Braelangwell and Newhall on the Black Isle. It may be noted that most of these, like a number east of Inverness, are situated in rich, agricultural districts where, whatever the upheavals of agricultural improvement, neither Clearance nor famine would much impinge.

Further south, old tower-houses fared differently under the influence of this classical taste in architecture. Castle Grant had a great, gaunt block grafted on to it, which Queen Victoria apparently said reminded her of a factory. Blair Castle, a substantial old building, was refashioned, perhaps with as much effort as at Foulis, in order to conform to classical norms, but the images I have seen of it look rather plain and not at all like the castle seen today.

Soon, the influence of the Romantic, which had so dominated the literature of the period, began to be seen in the architecture. In fact, it had been creeping in for a while; the huge, now partly demolished Gordon Castle, incorporating the older tower of Castle Gordon (strange, but true!), had miles of battlements foisted on its endless facades, in tribute to the older structure at its heart. And in 1802, its influence may have been felt again at Darnaway, where an old castle was removed, (apart, mercifully, from its Great Hall, complete with splendid 15th-century timber roof), being replaced by another symmetrical, classical mansion – except that it too had battlements and funny little turrets at the many corners. In 1805, Cluny Castle by Newtonmore received similar treatment, which could later be seen on the grandest scale at Taymouth in Perthshire. Some of these houses had flat roofs, a solution that is far from satisfactory in the Highland climate, and it is strange that they ever appeared on the wetter West Coast.

In Skye, on the more fertile, southern peninsula of Sleat, Lord MacDonald enlarged one of his numerous ancestral homes (though, to be fair, the sites of all the others were far more suited to clan warfare than elegant living). At Armadale, he already had a simple, modest house that still peeks out wistfully beyond the remains of the pile foisted on to it sometime after 1815. That section is now a pleasant ruin-cum-shrubbery, while the later central section, replaced apparently after a fire, has yet more battlements, square towers and a strange number of styles of window. Something of the same treatment was accorded to the ancestral home of the neighbouring MacLeods at Dunvegan, where a truly ancient site, furnished with towers, dungeon and hall, was admired by Sir Walter Scott when its owner had enveloped it in an even harling (now a sort of muddy brown), heightened the main tower (which, aesthetically, worked well) and provided the usual yards of battlement and occasional turret. Sadly, behind the battlements are expanses of flat roof, which leaked for decades and have only recently been made watertight, at great expense. Although it is often said that the Victorians used good materials when building, it is not so often realised that their architects had little clue of the worst the local climate could do!

It should perhaps be recorded that both Armadale and Dunvegan occupy truly beautiful sites, and have much to interest the visitor, whatever the merits or otherwise of their architecture.

Most of the above houses were built or drastically re-modelled by representatives of the ancient families that had lived on-site, sometimes for centuries. It was the Marquess of Breadalbane, for instance, a Campbell, who created the enormous Taymouth Castle, completed by the time of the first visit to Scotland by Queen Victoria and Prince Albert in 1842. When they went to Blair, that castle had been re-modelled by the Duke of Atholl, chief of Clan Murray, but did not look the way it does today. And at Ardverikie, the house they rented has also since disappeared. The visit to Ardverikie was in some ways different from the preceding two, as the house and estate had been let to the Duke of Abercorn by the owner, Cluny MacPherson, who was short of money. The Duke's own finances began to fail, and he sold the lease on… and on it went. The sporting estate had well and truly arrived, with it the new sporting proprietor and an endless chain of property deals.

The house that Victoria and Albert built for themselves at Balmoral has little of the militaristic splendour of Gordon Castle or Taymouth. It is so well known that most of us have its image in our minds and have given little thought to the elements that make it up. There is one tower, and it is substantial, but not otherwise particularly pretentious. There is also a house, again quite modest, and careful scrutiny of the popular views of the castle makes it clear that house and tower are almost separate. There are in fact two groups of buildings, the other being the stables and various offices, and the intention may have been for the strong vertical element of the tower to tie the two together. It is difficult to judge if this was a success as tall trees now limit the number of viewpoints of the buildings. As an architectural solution to a particular problem (the need to combine practical comfort and domestic convenience with more than a hint of history and nobility), the house-plus-tower arrangement was to prove very popular, although none of its protagonists built anything closely resembling Balmoral.

On a much smaller scale, and in comforting pink sandstone, the House of Aigas has similarities in that the southern elevation is of a symmetrical house to which, at one end, a tower has been attached. As happened elsewhere, the Victorian building was wrapped around a smaller predecessor. The result, as seen from the drive, was less successful than the south front until recent, tactful additions improved the balance of the whole composition. By this time (1877) we have a complete repertoire of architectural details: horizontal string-courses, bow windows, much corbelling, crow-step gables, finials, emphatic chimney stacks, and pepper pot or candle-snuffer type turrets, with cannon-style, fake drains. The upper windows have elaborate head-moulds, and stone shields hover in a number of places, ungraced by any coat-of-arms.

Where exactly do these elements come from? Most of them appear on the very important group of Scottish castles that have been dignified with the term 'Scots Baronial' (this being the case, the Victorian versions should properly, if clumsily, be called 'Neo-baronial'). These are the famous Castles of Mar, the best known of which are Crathes, Craigievar, Midmar and Fraser – with important 'outliers' (for various reasons) at Drum and Fyvie. The first four are notably *not* symmetrical, a feature that Victorian architects began increasingly to adopt, as they pursued the 'house-and-tower' theme. The height of the tower is important; if adequate, it could, as perhaps was the intention at Balmoral, provide a focal point for designs that were becoming increasingly disparate.

At Fairburn House, in Ross-shire (not far from Aigas), it seems to me that the architects did a good job; as seen from the entrance front, the complex massing works well, with the tower pulling the whole together. Something similar is achieved in the remoter Orcadian island of Shapinsay, where the substantial Balfour Castle is an equally intricate design. Ardverikie, again a truly large building, follows the Aigas arrangement, with a tower attached at one end of a symmetrical house. It does not work so well when viewed from the loch, but the tower is critical in balancing all the projections of the entrance front.

There can be no doubt that the view of 'one's new house' was important to most of these noble (or would-be-noble) owners, but few did it on the scale of the second Duke of Sutherland when enlarging the ancient seat of his mother's family at Dunrobin. The historic house here had been substantial before it was clasped by the huge additions designed by Sir Charles Barry, architect of the Houses of Parliament. At this time, the family used to arrive by sea, and Barry certainly ensured that they were greeted by an impressive sight. It is fortunate that this enormous building was generally well done, and that the proportions and details are quite delicate, sensitive and light in colour, so that it bears a considerable resemblance to a French palace, towering above its (now increasingly beautiful) formal gardens. When times changed, and the family started to arrive by rail – stopping at their own private station – the approach from this direction, although dignified by a complex avenue of trees, lacked impact in comparison with that from the water. The big tower here, part of Barry's design, was later damaged by fire and somewhat re-modelled by Sir Robert Lorimer, who also recast some of the interior. There is, however, really no complete landward facade; apparently, plans exist which, if built, would have remedied that lack, while adding yet more to the existing structure. It is, I think, no secret that the current incumbent is very pleased that his ancestor never built this projected new wing.

Another later building was large and extremely French in style: Rosehaugh on the Black Isle. Building started in 1893 of what was one of the most elaborate, visually, of all these houses. In particular it had: prominent, high roofs; very complex fenestration; and encrusted dormers, gables and spires. The interior was supposedly equally opulent, with a swimming pool and Turkish baths.

Despite their size and complex detailing, both Dunrobin and Rosehaugh displayed a lightness of touch that was denied to one of the remotest of these incredible, seasonal hunting lodges. On the Inner Hebridean Isle of Rum, Sir George Bullough built for himself the remarkable Kinloch Castle. Work started in 1897 on a structure that, like others mentioned, possesses long, unconvincing battlements and corner turrets. Again, like others, it has a main tower, sufficient perhaps to justify the use of the word 'castle' (this is not on the site of any ancient stronghold). But it belongs to the 'house-plus-tower' group, and the architects chose to place the tower off-centre, rising out of a long, otherwise somewhat monotonous facade. In front of this, again laden with irrelevant battlements, is one feature that is both original and practical, given the wet climate of the island: a covered walkway. The weather in Rum, which can be atrocious, has unfortunately made a nonsense of all these long battlements, which conceal and limit the gutters behind them. They have often proved quite inadequate to cope with the regular deluges and have overflowed, sending the surplus water down into the interior of the building, with unfortunate, if inevitable, results.

Truth be told, these elaborate Victorian houses, varying in scale and architectural pretension, are found in what seem the most unlikely of locations throughout the Highlands and Islands, from Amhuinnsuidhe on the shore of western Harris to Vaila in Shetland and, in the Highlands, from the empty moors of Caithness where Lochdhu Lodge breaks the endless horizons, to Old Corrour in its inaccessible wilds (now replaced by a spectacular modern building some four storeys in height). They appear out of nowhere up the least frequented of glens. If you are not aware of their existence, the impact of their improbable architecture, often looming out of the mist, is considerable. I well recall my first sight of the tall tower of Glencassley, appearing above the gloomy Scots pines on a day of torrential rain in its long, largely empty, Sutherland glen.

The water from the River Cassley, joining that of the Oykell, flows eastward into the Kyle of Sutherland, and ultimately below the bulk of one of the latest of the series, Carbisdale Castle. It too has a conspicuous tower, like Ardverikie and others, rather off to one side of the substantial main house, which is best seen from across the wide river. Construction began in 1906, just out of, and looking across at, lands belonging to the Duke of Sutherland, from whose family the builder, the apparently unpopular widow of the third Duke, was estranged. Complicated then, its subsequent history has been varied: during the Nazi occupation of Norway in World War II, it served as a safe refuge for King Haakon VII and King Olav V. It was later a popular youth hostel, giving visitors from all over the world a memorable base for a night or two.

The sheer scale of these Victorian buildings, along with the weather prevailing in the Highlands and Islands, and the fact that few of them were occupied throughout the year, have led to many problems of upkeep and repair. If you consider a building like Ardverikie, or Balfour, which have roofs of great complexity, with so many valleys and ridges, then the problems of construction and maintenance are little less than daunting. It is little wonder that a number have, like Rosehaugh, been demolished, or that Victorian wings were often quite happily flattened. Some families must be very glad that grand Victorian plans for their home, ancestral or otherwise, never came to fruition. I think particularly of Cawdor, where Victorian additions are modest and in keeping with the rest. At Foulis, twenty-four years of pointless family litigation led to much of the estate being sold but, in retrospect, this at least spared the current family the possibility of having to maintain some huge Victorian pile. Some have been restored at great expense: Ardross Castle, an extravagant building in itself, being one of the most notable examples.

In passing, a few other houses should probably be mentioned, mainly because their architects (or owners) decided not to follow the fashion for these great, towered houses, and chose instead a rather English, half-timbered, domestic style, which generally looks somewhat out of place. Remote Wyvis Lodge is one of these, Mar Lodge on Deeside being significantly larger. The owners of both houses were people of interest: Mar was built by the Duke and Duchess of Fife. She was a grand-daughter of Queen Victoria and apparently chose the architectural style herself. Can she possibly have had enough of the tower and turrets of Balmoral? And Wyvis belonged to the Shoolbred family, renowned cabinet-makers who, naturally, provided their own furniture.

Some houses, like Armadale and Kinloch, were simply abandoned, with damp affecting the interiors and contents. The latter retains much of its original furnishings, brought from all over the globe to this remote location, and its undeniable splendour is a good example of the type. There was certainly an overall tendency to sombre grandeur: dark wood, whether in furniture or doors, skirting-boards, banisters and panelling (acres of it!) set the tone. It is fortunate, perhaps, that the windows of most of these houses were large enough to let some light in, as many of the portraits hanging on the walls were also pretty sombre. Where the walls were coloured rather than panelled, the colours were often strong but, again, dark. Greens and reds were often used, the latter lending richness to the two-storeyed hall of Kinloch; it also features in Balfour. Despite the fact that there is a portrait of Sir George Bullough in his kilt, Kinloch is not much adorned with tartan – unlike many others. Most surfaces seem to have been patterned, some are extraordinarily ornate, and where original interiors survive, there was no shortage of ornaments.

Not all had grand entrance halls in the style of Kinloch (with a grand piano and almost barbaric Oriental statues and figurines). Aigas has a smaller hall, still impressive and now used for dining, but both were simply reception rooms, places where the family might gather before dinner. Both Balfour and Kinloch had fine drawing rooms where a more feminine style prevailed, with very light wallpaper and far less dark wood. In both, the men could head for the billiard room; that at Balfour is some distance from the main rooms, while at Kinloch it opens off the hall, and is firmly a billiard-cum-smoking room, with special ventilation provided. The royal houses had ball-rooms, although as something perhaps of an afterthought: that at Balmoral is at least attached to the main building, but at Mar you have to go outside to get access. More convenient by far is that of Kinloch (where I have danced – the floor is well sprung). A few houses had chapels, that at Balfour being relatively small and modest. Libraries are common but vary drastically in size: Balfour's is large and well-stocked, while the Aigas version is significantly smaller.

Private bathrooms were fairly unusual in such houses, although Lady Monica Bullough ensured that she had one at Balfour. There were long corridors of bedrooms, with occasional bathrooms. I have been lucky enough to stay in Kinloch on numerous occasions and have slept in a number of the bedrooms, most of them fairly sombre, with dark, normally rather short, four-posters. But one very large corner room in Kinloch is not only well-lit but contained a bed that could, I estimate, easily have slept four (no, we did not!).

The plumbing is one of the constant delights in such houses.

At Kinloch the bath-cum-shower arrangement looks like a sentry box installed at the tap end of a very long, high-sided bath. The sentry box contains the shower, with a shower-head about six inches across. Various settings were at your service, and most made an impact: one came up from the floor of the bath and could almost lift you off your feet, another sent painful jets hard at your naked body from the surrounding sides of the sentry box. You were supposed to be able to have waves in your bath, but this was never working in my time. By far the most memorable I have ever seen, however, was in a bathroom in that simply incredible building, Mount Stuart on Bute. This seems to have been sub-divided into cubicles containing the usual amenities: in one, there stands a bidet, robustly labelled (elegant script on a brass-plate, to be sure) 'bottom shower' – just in case you did not know.

Some owners collected old portraits, or displayed those of their own family, but commissioned landscapes of their estates were just as common. Those of Rum all seem to have been painted in blazing sunshine, perhaps simply to torment the guests when they experienced the more normal summer weather of the island. Sporting landscapes were popular, as were paintings of the objects of their sport, whether grouse, ptarmigan, leaping salmon or noble stags. Bits of these creatures, like grouse claws or red deer hooves, were mounted in silver, attached to polished wood and scattered around the house. Birds shot on the estate and fish caught in the rivers were stuffed and located in the principal rooms. But, of course, it was deer that could be seen in the greatest abundance – at least their stuffed heads, sometimes simply the antlers. These were everywhere, especially along passages and up stairways; all the stairs at Mar Lodge, for instance, seem to have them, mounted in ranks, mournful eyes reproaching you every time you move anywhere in the building.

One must remember that these are the trappings of a cult, and the caste that embraced it, as well as being the raison d'être of the whole vast edifice. This is what it was about, and modern sensibilities are irrelevant. It is, however, hard to remember this when you first enter the doors of the ballroom at Mar Lodge. As far as one can see, the beams, the rest of the roof and some of the walls of this vast room are festooned with the antlers of countless stags. I say 'countless' because it never even occurred to me to count them, but I read that the building contains the skulls and antlers of 2,435 stags. The effect is totally overwhelming and, it has to be said, to many, appalling.

Some may think that I, and others, are overreacting here, which is fine. But what must be taken on board is the scale of the sporting cult that produced these extraordinary lodges in their remote locations. The Mar Lodge Ballroom makes clear the reality of that passion and, I think, comprehensible the effect it had on the Highlands.

Eight

A WALK IN RUM

I am in the island of Rum for a few days, with a small group of folk. We have already had two very pleasant days, although yesterday evening, low mist robbed us of the chance to go up to the shearwater colony at night. I was very suspicious that today we would find the mist had descended to sea level, but it has not. The sky is wonderfully blue, a light breeze keeps the dreaded Rum midges at bay, and we can leave the sheltered Kinloch policies at a dignified pace – I have, on previous occasions, had to run until we were out of the trees.

Accordingly, we turn up the track that leads into the heart of the island. It may once have deserved the title of 'road', when Sir George Bullough is said to have kept a couple of fine cars and raced across to Harris Bay. Now, however, 'track' is a much more apt description. It is not narrow, but exceptionally rough and, after a while, hard on the feet. We get ourselves into a reasonable rhythm, walking with the medium-sized burn, which has sometimes been dignified with the name of Kinloch River, on our right. It is exceptionally pretty in the sun, its small, rock-edged pools overhung with the occasional slender birch, growing amid the blooming bell-heather.

All around us the trees are young, as we are walking in a very large plantation that has not yet reached maturity. Rum is owned by Scottish Natural Heritage and has been dedicated to nature conservation since its predecessor body purchased it from the Bullough family. In fact, it might be more accurate to say that the island has been largely dedicated to two, often opposed, aspects of the natural heritage. Most of the effort has gone into studying a large herd of red deer, and to planting trees in an area from which the deer were excluded many years ago. When the Nature Conservancy Council arrived on the island, there was almost no natural woodland left apart from a few remnants on the sheltered southern shore of Loch Scresort, the sea loch on the eastern coast, at the head of which stands Kinloch. Here, too, the Bulloughs and their predecessors had done some amenity planting, creating the woodland shelter around the houses, which is now such a tangle of sycamore and rhododendron, with pine on the outer fringes. But there are many other exotics lurking in there, including bamboo and eucalyptus. The policy, since, has been to create a significant woodland spreading out from the shelter of Kinloch Glen, using mostly, pine, birch, rowan and alder. In a few places, their growth has begun to modify the vegetation around the trees, permitting the appearance of woodland flowers, but in others, large swathes of trees are noticeably heading towards the stage at which they should be thinned, without any change to the underlying, rough moorland grasses and occasional patches of heather. Planting the trees on Rum (over a million are said to have been planted) is, it would seem, only half the battle; creating woodland will take hugely longer – if it happens at all. Regular visits over twenty years, all involving trekking out along this same route, have shown remarkably little change, except in the height of the trees.

We reach the big gates in the fence and let ourselves out into the open country. As we walk along the track, there is a significant escarpment on our left. I keep glancing up at it, in case an eagle should appear above us. If we could take wings and fly up over the escarpment, we would find ourselves on something of a plateau, an area of rough moorland with a number of attractive lochs of different sizes. I often say that both Eigg (we were there earlier in the week) and Rum have their own 'Lake District' – a rocky, hilly area with many bodies of water. They are quite different in appearance, however, and we had fun walking up there in Rum's version yesterday. There are red-throated divers on the smaller lochs, and we had some wonderful views. Today, a couple fly overhead on their way to feed in the sea, their distinctive harsh cackle an aid to rapid identification.

After a while, there is a junction in our track, and I lead my small group first along the branch that heads to the left and, ultimately, down to the west coast of the island and the lovely bay of Harris, which we had looked at from on high while walking the wonderful ridge of Barkeval only yesterday. We are not really going to the coast, but I enjoy being mysterious and will not tell them yet why we are heading in, apparently, the wrong direction. We stop for a while by a stone bridge, enjoy a quick cup of coffee and rest our feet while continuously looking around – for anything! Today, it all seems very quiet.

As we gain a little height, we begin to see more of the glen that runs to the north, to Kilmory, where, ultimately, we mean to go. That glen appears almost straight and flows from a loch that is also fairly straight – it is called the Long Loch. This distinct line, from the loch down the glen, marks a geological fault. Up to now, since the gate in the deer-fence, and apart from the stony surface of our track and the recent bridge, there has been hardly a sign of the hand of man, but in a little while we reach a point where it can be quite clearly seen that some-one, at some stage, has been trying to do something significant in the landscape.

Down on our right across a deep hollow are the very obvious remains of a big, stone dam. At this point, we are in a wide-open space between hills. But this is a wet island, and a lot of water flows from these hills; two burns come together at this point and, once joined, have been dammed. From beside the dam, stony lines head east. These mark a cutting that was meant to take this water towards the burn flowing to Kinloch, diverting it away from Kilmory, to which it naturally would have continued. As we stand there, we can see that the Long Loch itself was dammed at its far end, raising the level until the water from there could flow through another cutting, almost a small canal, along the hill behind us, again to join the east-flowing burn. These two dams were built by an earlier owner, Lord Salisbury, in order to create a more significant river flowing to Kinloch. After all that work, it is said that the dam only lasted two days before it burst, and sent a great surge of water down to Kilmory. So ended Lord Salisbury's extraordinary efforts to have salmon running in his river, increasing not only the sporting activities available in his island but also its prestige. His existing streams had autumnal runs of small sea trout, like those I had fished for in the Leraig, so there was a little sport to be had. But he dreamed of greater things. He managed, no doubt, to bag some grouse, but the wetlands of the West are not good for them and numbers can never have approached that of the eastern moors. Yesterday, in all our walking, we heard one.

From here, we head back to the junction and follow the long road to Kilmory, down the glen we have already seen. There are a few, smaller plantations along it, adding a little variety to the birdlife. But, in all honesty, the walk feels a little monotonous as we stride northwards. There are some damp ruts in the track, which is softer in places here, and our way is enlivened by a number of dragonflies, including the large golden-ringed, which rustle here and there like tiny helicopters.

At last the track rises slightly and we can see that we are reaching a more open and fertile area, with several field-walls and the remains of some structures. This is Kilmory, a name ('church of Mary') indicating that it was, for a long time, an important place in the island, although its fertility would have guaranteed that people lived here, anyway. Down towards the sea is what should really be machair grassland, studded with wildflowers, but we can see a number of hinds and their calves, and it is all, we discover later, highly overgrazed. I do actually manage to find a few examples of one of my favourite flowers, the delicate Grass of Parnassus, but that is about it. Despite the fact that this is a National Nature Reserve and such grassland, botanically important as it is, is not exactly common in Rum, it seems that Kilmory's machair is of far less significance to SNH than the large expanse of planted woodland, or the herd of deer.

At this point, the SNH study area, within which deer are supreme, is mostly over to our west. For over forty years, deer have been closely observed, tracked, counted and culled, and while some of the conclusions may not be all that surprising (like the idea that culling hind numbers is the best way to regulate the population), other bits of information emerging from the study have been counter to old ideas (like the fact that few stags live to be more than thirteen years old). This is, however, a fairly tough environment for deer, despite the fertility of some of the soils. Deer are fundamentally woodland animals and, while they can obviously adapt to far poorer conditions, all ruminants suffer badly in constant wet, wind and cold – which sounds very like the description of the average Rum winter.

We find some splendid rocks to sit on for lunch, looking over a tranquil sea to the south end of Skye and the massed Black Cuillin hills. Gulls fly by, and a few gannets. A ferry passes, then some common seals, playful in the turquoise water.

We sit quiet after our sandwiches, enjoying the view, some dozing, others looking for small waders – ringed plovers, perhaps – in the shingle at the river mouth. It is a lovely place.

After a while, I point out a building over beyond us, used now for the deer study project. It was formerly the laundry for the castle when the Bulloughs owned the island. The estimates I have seen of the distance for the round trip here and back vary, but it is at least eleven miles – which is one way of ensuring that your fellow guests don't see your underclothes on the line! By now, it has become really quite warm, and I propose that we have an hour to ourselves before we start the long walk back. A few decide to linger where they are, while one or two of us think that the tranquil water looks tempting, and head across the denuded machair to the other side of the bay in order to enjoy a distant skinny-dip. This turns out not only to be tactful but brief as the water is predictably cold. I run around on the pink sand for a while to warm up again, then dress and rejoin the others.

In the interval, more hinds and calves have appeared, and it does make for a pleasant scene as the well-fed animals, with their rich, red summer coats, graze on the short turf. I suppose it could be said that they represent Lord Salisbury's greatest success in his efforts to turn the 'cleared' island into a prestigious sporting estate. Probably quite some time before he purchased the island, the native population of small deer had been hunted out. They must always have been fairly few in order for the human population to carry on its vital agriculture at Harris, Kilmore and Kinloch, and the other, smaller isolated settlements like Papadil. Lord Salisbury had to reintroduce deer from outside, and let the population build up before he could start to stalk the stags, let alone take a few hinds in the winter. When you add into the picture Sir George's extraordinary expenditure on the castle and its furnishings, the planting of the extensive policies with the gardens they sheltered, and all the rest of it, Rum can easily be seen, along with Mar Lodge and its ballroom, as one of the greatest monuments to the Victorian sporting culture.

As for us, we have to turn our backs on Kilmory and face what does seem like the long walk home. It becomes hard work after a while, and we are mostly silent but when we turn to look back to the sun over the sea, there are two great, dark shapes gliding across the glen in the silence of the early evening. It is hard to make out exactly what they are, till one turns, and its white tail briefly catches the light; these are while-tailed sea eagles and Rum was one of the sites chosen for their reintroduction to the West Coast of Scotland. They had been hunted by gamekeepers throughout the 1800s finally becoming extinct in 1916. That, too, was part of the sporting culture.

Nine

THE GARDENS OF
THE BIG HOUSES

The builders of the new houses did not envisage them towering over an otherwise empty landscape, although that is how
they, and often their successors, must really have known them.
We have seen that even before the Victorians, in the wilds
of Assynt, gardens were created around both the stark tower
of Ardvreck, and the symmetrical mansion that replaced it,
Calda House. The planting of trees not native to the Highlands
(or rarely found there, like the yew) clearly goes back well
before the advent of the sporting estate. On the West Coast,
the sheltered area at the head of Little Loch Broom around
Dundonnell House is given great serenity by the presence of a
considerable number of wonderful old trees, including several
sweet chestnuts, and an amazing yew in the formal gardens.
On the East Coast, Cawdor was likewise embellished over a
long period, not only on the fringes of the Big Wood, but, for
instance, around the old church of Barevan, where in a corner
of the churchyard, another sweet chestnut, multi-stemmed and
wide-spreading, still appears in the best of health.

  This wonderful tendency, to beautify the landscape with fine
trees, was a hugely important part of the culture of the Victorian
period in the Highlands, and one we should be very grateful for.

In an era of rather instant gardening, when trees of quite some size may easily be purchased and planted in order to create, very rapidly, the vision of the gardener, it is worth remembering that this is not how it used to be done. Although Walter Grant, Laird of Rousay, was not the first to plant trees around his tall mansion of Trumland, he carried on the tradition, and when my grand-mother visited in the 1930s, she was asked, when walking, to be very careful not to tread on the young trees he had planted; the estate staff had not yet finished the mowing around the saplings in the long grass, which hid a number of them. This was plant-ing for the future, with no personal hope of ever seeing anything like the mature trees of today.

Almost every one of the big houses was provided with extensive amenity grounds – or policies – and they are often conspicuous because of the size and variety of trees planted, contained perhaps within a wall, or substantial metal fence. The great era of exploration, when ornithologists, biologists and botanists (and goodness knows who else) crossed the globe bringing back specimens of all kinds, resulted in an explosion of interest in foreign trees, and the discovery that many of them would grow rather well in Britain, and particularly well in Scotland, where the area around the inner Moray Firth, and much of Tayside, feature among the best tree-growing areas in Europe. Some, like the beech and sycamore, were simply brought north, where although now regarded by the purists of Scottish Natural Heritage as exotic and undesirable, they have flourished and, especially in the Outer and Northern Isles, grow better than almost anything else. The big planta-tions, for instance, around Binscarth and Balfour in Orkney, and Lews Castle by Stornoway, all started with sycamore, and still provide the largest areas of sheltered woodland there. But many, rather more exotic trees will be found in extensive pol-icies: spruces, both Norway and Sitka, Douglas and grand fir, giant sequoia, European larch, red and turkey oak, and perhaps most decorative of all, the splendid copper beeches. Some have grown rather faster in the Highlands than they do in their home countries, which means, sadly, that a number are beginning to die back – but again, many landowners are, wonderfully, still planting new arboretums for the future.

The creation of picturesque landscapes sometimes extended for quite a distance from the big house; an estate village would also be embellished with specimen trees, a sheltered glen like that of Reelig or Plodda would be similarly adorned, and provided with well-constructed walks. At Plodda, a small burn was even diverted quite some distance, so that it might fall over the edge of the gorge and provide a spectacular feature in the already impressive landscape. The place now known as The Hermitage, in Perthshire, where the River Braan tumbles between suitably rugged rocks, was provided with a rustic arched bridge and a folly. Within the policies around Kinloch in Rum, another burn was diverted so that it flowed close to the house, and was embellished with decorative bridges. Bushes were often planted, with, on occasion, results that the gardeners had clearly never anticipated. In the acid soils of much of the Highlands, it turned out that rhododendrons flourished, while in the richer soils of Orkney, it was salmonberry. Both are now frequently regarded as a pest, with a lot of effort going into removing them. The most common rhododendron, *R. ponticum*, has spread significantly on to the open hillsides in parts of Mull and on the shores of Loch Torridon, while it has completely taken over the understorey of many wooded areas, spectacularly, for instance around Plockton. The salmonberry has done exactly the same on Rousay, and when I last tried to walk it, the burnside path through the policies had become an impassable jungle.

It is hard, however, in a Highland spring, for many of us to disapprove totally of *R. ponticum* when it brings colour to a

landscape that is otherwise still dead. It is also true that gardens
of specimen azaleas and rhododendrons are a significant feature
in the Highlands. Osgood MacKenzie, who created the famous
gardens at Inverewe in Wester Ross, may well have started this
trend, but he must have been one of the few who actually was
there to see his gardens in flower, as so many of the sporting
lodges were only occupied in the late summer and early autumn.
Despite this, some acquired grand formal gardens, often walled,
as at Dunrobin and Balfour, the latter now undergoing a thorough restoration. The growing of vegetables and fruit for the big
house during its period of occupation was widespread, and the
planting of fruit trees against south-facing walls made it possible
to grow successfully an astonishing variety in the open air; it
makes one wonder why this habit has not been continued on a
suitably smaller scale. Large greenhouses grew all sorts of exot-
ica, too, with vines at both Trumland and Balfour.

Such policies and gardens might be provided with a number
of special features: fountains and ponds; flights of stone steps;
follies; decorative summerhouses or outlook towers; sundi-
als; or even pet cemeteries with tombstones. Queen Victoria
added several memorial cairns to the grounds around Balmoral,
where one could, presumably, indulge in gloomy reflection;
the rather more cheerful intention of simply enjoying a splendid view over the islands was thwarted at Trumland when
the small eminence intended for the location of a garden seat
turned out to be a little chambered tomb, of Neolithic date and
unique in Britain, owing to its two storeys.

In some places, complete landscapes were planned and if an
old settlement was going to interfere with the desired view, it
might well be simply relocated, as at Guisachan (on the way up
to Plodda). At Balfour, the new village was planned as part of
the approach to the castle, and the view from the sea to both
was made more picturesque by the addition of an interesting

structure, which looks rather like an early lighthouse and incorporated both a doocot (or dovecote) and a seawater shower.

In addition to the policies around the big house, individual specimen trees, copses and larger groups were planted in more open landscapes; where they survive, they are often most impressive. On Royal Deeside, for instance, around the towered establishment of Invercauld, the designed landscape – with the river winding through open grassland embellished with several splendid trees, many of them larches, backed by denser plantations and the open hill – is extremely fine.

On a number of these estates, the smaller buildings often somehow appear the most fantastical. Some of the greater houses went in for entrance lodges or gate-houses in a big way. Dunrobin has a good example, while Ardverikie, not content with a magnificent bridge, boasts a building beside it that could well have been designed for Ludwig II of Bavaria. Castle Grant has one that is rather cleverly attached to the railway line in a way which makes it rather more impressive than it would otherwise be. Estate cottages often have their own architectural features; some, like the elaborate external woodwork of many in Tomich (approaching the very ruined, rather Italianate Guisachan House), must be very fiddly to keep painted as often as is required in the wet Highland climate. And the latticed windows must also be a real nuisance to keep clean.

There are many places in the Highlands where several of these distinctive features remain, often in locations not featuring high on the list of tourist destinations. Easter Ross is a very distinct part of that county, far less visited than the West Coast and, if anything, the countryside where it adjoins the plateau-mountain of Ben Wyvis and its northerly neighbours (in other words, its western limit) is even less frequented. I am thinking of Ardross, where recently, one summer day, I took my car up the remarkably straight road towards the head of Strath Rusdale. This road lies on the northern, sunny side of the gentle valley, and while the hilltops are planted with conifers, the gentle slopes beneath them are noticeably fertile and well-farmed. The big fields, straight-sided, are typical of the Victorian agricultural revolution and, before you have driven far up the road, a stylish sandstone cottage, immaculately kept, gives the game away: you are entering the grounds of a large Victorian estate. There are still trees along the road and between several of the fields, and, after a while, there is an area across the waters of the River Averon that resembles southern parkland, an expanse of sweeping grass and big trees. Along this road, you pass neat farm cottages, a substantial farm, the extensive policy-woodlands and magnificent gates, with fine cast-iron railings on either side. The gate gives access to a lovely avenue leading to the 'big house', which is invisible from the road but, as Ardross Castle fortunately advertises itself as a venue for weddings and conferences, many photographs of its undoubted splendour are in the public domain. Its complex sandstone facade, complete with towers and *porte-cochère*, bow-windows and turrets, and possibly the most exuberant crow-step gables I have ever seen, conceals fine reception rooms, including a huge hall with a glorious painted ceiling, and a chapel – complete with Byzantine art.

All this glory apparently began as a 'modest Munro house' that was ultimately transformed by Charles William Dyson Perrins, who bought the place in 1880. The sporting estate of which it was the heart (if far from the geographical centre) once extended over the hills to Glencalvie, scene of those Clearances in 1845, and the two were connected by a long, well-built private road, which passes through some fairly bleak uplands, but enabled Dyson Perrins to visit the far-flung limits of his estate without going off his own land. He was typical enough of these new proprietors (although it is hard to comprehend that quite so much money could actually be made by making and selling sauce): he was generous to the community, 'quiet and unassuming' and apparently regarded as 'delightful and good-hearted' by the Scots poet Hugh MacDiarmid, who for a while worked with his wife on the estate. MacDiarmid was effectively communist in outlook, and Dyson Perrins owned countless thousands of Highland acres, so it is a most remarkable tribute.

Ten

A WALK IN STRATHSPEY

It is autumn now and when we start, quite promptly, this morning there is a frost under the trees around the Field Centre and mist over the still waters of the Beauly Firth. We come quite briskly south from Inverness along the busy A9, but leave it at Aviemore and head up towards the great, sculpted plateau of the Cairngorms. Loch Morlich is totally calm, dark and sombre, reflecting the woods of pine and the almost-black hills, but the scene is part-veiled by strands of the softest and whitest of mists, which lends it pure enchantment. We stop, inevitably, to admire and to photograph and to look for some birds on the water – just in case. The only reward is a dozen mallard.

A little further on, we park on the verge, close to the Reindeer Centre, and get ourselves organised for a walk in the woods above. It is very much a case of ensuring that we have the hats and gloves that we need; the air is still cold and, although the sky is clearing, the sun is not yet reaching us.

Our way lies uphill, first on a tarred road past the Centre and a couple of houses, then swinging right on to a good forestry track with quite a pleasant gradient for walking; you know that you are walking uphill, gaining height, but only need the occasional halt to help you catch your breath. On our right for quite a while is a mature plantation of exotic conifers with fine specimens on the edge, and beyond, the dark, dense sterility of an un-thinned, un-snedded stand of immensely tall trunks. There seems to be no vegetation beneath them, apart from a scattering of somewhat repellent, pallid fungi.

On our left the trees are younger, presumably replacing a similar, but now felled, plantation. This has been replanted at different times and is not only of differing age, but varying composition. Some parts are single-species, but native this time – Scots pine with its distinctive reddish bark. Other compartments have experienced regeneration, perhaps even planting, of some native deciduous trees, with the autumn colours of birch and rowan. In places, though, the prickly spruces have seeded and are also growing well, and are rather past the stage when they should have been eliminated if the aim is to make a new native woodland. Creating something that actually resembles a native woodland requires a lot more labour than is normally made available and once exotics get a hold, they are very hard to remove. Most of this is unfenced as all of it is old enough to withstand the depredations of deer, but one section of fence can be seen and rather mystifies us: it is the full height of a deer fence, made of a quite visible black plastic netting, and runs parallel to our track for a while. We understand the visibility all right – it is in order to avoid too many birds flying into it and breaking their necks – but its overall purpose remains unclear. It is a single, straight length, making no effort to enclose anything, with no sign that it has ever been attached to any other sort of barrier. Nor is it echoed on the other side of the track.

But there are other things to consider as we walk uphill: one or two ant-hills, rather quiet on this cold morning; some pine-marten droppings on the gravel at the side; late pink flowers on the cowberry plants of the woodland banks; blaeberry leaves turning orange and red; birds to listen for and try to find in the canopy high above our heads. Some siskins jangle way up there, and a mixed flock of tits passes by at a lower level enabling us to make out blue and great tits, and the lovely, tiny, delicate long-tails.

After a reasonable walk, the track begins to level out, running straight between well-established plantations of Scots pine; on the right, there are a few of the much older 'granny pines', madly multi-stemmed and strangely shaped, to the extent that a generation of foresters decided they were inferior and should not be allowed to regenerate. If such trees were not actually felled, they were planted densely around (sometimes with stock from German sources), acres of which have since been felled and the brash left to rot.

We discuss the pros and cons of this and other forestry policies, standing around in the very welcome sunshine. Shortly after the granny pines, the scene opens out significantly, mainly as the result of what must have been a serious fire ripping its way through the dense trees. As a result, there are good views towards the dark, rounded mountains, so we scan along the skyline – and our reward is a distant golden eagle, a young one, starkly black-and-white in the brilliant light. High up there would be mountain hares, the blue hares (in reality more greyish in colour) sometimes rather obvious if they stray into the dark brown of thick heather, and they make a good meal for a hungry eagle facing its first winter in the frozen hills. At this stage, in mid-October, the hares have presumably not yet taken on their white winter coats; if they had, they would be as conspicuous in the heather as a stoat I once saw, pristine in its winter ermine, running along the seaweed of an Assynt shore.

We come to a stop here and have quite a lively debate as to whether it makes sense to use public money to plant pines of European origin, and then to use more public money to destroy them, in case, in some way, they contaminate our Highland landscapes by hybridising with the local specimens. Would the offspring of such illicit unions be more vulnerable, or stronger? What about 'hybrid vigour', asks a gardener in the group

– a very good question, too. When our native species seem to be increasingly at the mercy of exotic pests, *Phytophthera* and so on, does it make any sense that our policy seems to be to defend the almost-Aryan purity of our own stock, even though we may have to watch it being decimated within a few decades? And do the exotics really matter so much? Just downhill from us, having seeded itself into the zone cleared by the fire is a red *Sambucus*, a plant that crops up in the most unexpected locations, far from any seed source, perhaps carried by (or in) migrating birds.

Eventually, I call a halt to the debate, and we continue on our way. Here the whole scene changes – and so does the track. It is now very much a Highland path, constantly changing direction, uphill and downhill, obstructed by rocks and crossed by numerous roots, treacherous if wet. Having dutifully warned my group to go carefully and take it gently, we venture along it. Early on, there is an enormous, complex pine, sadly now greatly reduced by a storm, with enough remaining, however, to give some idea of its original might. There are other old pines, too, but also juniper all around and lots of youngish deciduous trees; again birch and rowan, one of the latter with leaves of flame and heavy-laden with scarlet berries, a brave sight in the sunshine. There are also willows, and quite a lot of dark, glossy hollies – some will, in their turn, be brilliant with berries by Christmas. A few alder provide a note of sobriety, and there is just enough bracken to add its russet to the range of colours around us. As we walk slowly through this very different place, I am listening carefully, and we eventually hear the call of a crested tit. For once it does not stay high above us, and we have a quick view of its jaunty profile as it investigates the complex bark of another old pine. Honeysuckle grows up off the woodland floor, and some way off the track, ivy is inching its way up the silver stems of a couple of birches.

This is the genuine article, the 'native woodland', even the authentic 'Caledonian Pine Forest': a mixed habitat of great richness, healthy, most species visibly regenerating. As we walk along the path, I stop at intervals to point out a number of rather unexpected plants, none in flower now, of course, but their leaves quite clear – and significant. These include wood sanicle, sweet woodruff, dog's mercury, all plants that you might expect to find in an undisturbed, deciduous woodland in the Highlands, indicating the diverse nature of this wonderful place. Apart from these, there are the more usual berry plants, the blaeberry and cowberry we had already seen further down. These berries are, of course, quite important feeding for a number of species, especially for one bird in particular.

The capercaillie, the great forest grouse, does inhabit such woodlands, but the chances of seeing it seem to grow ever less. It is more general in where it chooses to live than many people think, being far from restricted to the 'old Caledonian Pine Forest', or even to Scots pine trees. It used to be found in the plantations of the Black Isle, and I have seen it near Guisachan among spruce and larch and other exotics. I have never had the intimidating encounters one used to read of during the years when they were more common – Land Rovers or walkers attacked by these apoplectic, turkey-sized creatures – but a male did fly low over my head once when I was wandering well off the beaten track in the woods behind Loch an Eilein one autumn day. And I also cherish the memory of a distant martial silhouette, seen through binoculars on a frosty, golden dawn.

It is generally stated that the capercaillie became extinct in Scotland in the late 1700s. The populations of some birds are generally less stable than others, and grouse seem to be particularly prone to catastrophic changes, so this should be borne in mind throughout the ensuing discussion. Climatic change, if it be towards cold, wet springs, does them few favours, by reducing the insects on which the chicks are dependent, while increasing their need for nourishment to resist the cold. It is hard to establish when the European cold spell, commonly known as the Little Ice Age, actually ended (or how) in precise localities, but it may well have involved a prolonged spell of cold, wet springs and the dates seem, roughly, to fit. There was quite an area of suitable habitat left in Scotland at this period, except that, as I remarked earlier, much of it must have been pasture-woodland with, presumably, substantially less vegetation on the woodland floor than we would now look for. This would make these ground-nesting birds rather vulnerable to predation, and as this period is well before the wholesale vendetta of the organised Victorian gamekeeper, there must have been more predators than there were after the birds were reintroduced (and for a long time, perhaps up to the outbreak of the Great War). Although there were, effectively, plenty of suitable woods, they were clearly beginning to suffer from depredations by the growing local populations, and some experienced significant felling by external contractors, as was the case in those woods by Loch Maree and Loch Lomond, and in Rothiemurchus, Glen Affric and Strath Farrar. This felling created real disturbance, encouraging the regeneration of fallen pine-cones, which resulted in the older trees we now see in such places, but the disturbance itself may have been a significant factor in reducing yet further the number of capercaillie.

All these factors, anyway, may have been enough to eliminate the native population. Precisely because of the new sporting culture, the capercaillie was reintroduced from Sweden in the 1830s, and initially the birds appear to have flourished in the predator-free environment of the period. People began to shoot them, so they also appear in the halls of the lodges, stuffed and belligerent in pose. The RSPB website suggests that from a high of around 20,000 birds as recently as 1970, numbers have fallen drastically to around 1,285 birds in winter 2009/10, some thirty per cent down from winter 2003/04. Once again, folk want to know what is going on; why this astonishing decline in the numbers of one of the few birds to deserve that overused description of 'iconic'?

At this point, one might re-read the last paragraph but one. Grouse are prone to serious fluctuations in numbers. Climatic change could be a factor and a whole series of springs has been cold and wet; we used to encourage visitors to come to the Highlands and Islands in late spring and early summer, when we could rely on having some of the best weather of the year, but a warm and dry May or June is a rarity these days. There is no shortage of suitable habitat unless, for some reason, capercaillie need old trees; if they do, there is little we can do but wait. They presumably benefit from a relatively ungrazed woodland floor, covered in berries, but reducing deer numbers should achieve that relatively easily. They are still nesting on the ground, and must be very prone to disturbance, and there are certainly far more predators around than there were when I was young. We are so happy to see increased numbers of otters, pine martens and badgers (and, apparently, many people are worried about the status of the wildcat), but the increase in their visibility must come at some substantial cost to all birds that nest on the ground.

In addition, the landscape inhabited by these birds has changed a lot in the intervening couple of centuries; worried by a decline in native woodland, people have been planting lots of new ones, and because of the great increase in the number of deer, these new plantations have had to be securely fenced. We have discovered since, of course, that all grouse have difficulty in seeing the strung wires, and regularly fly into them, often killing themselves. Accordingly, all new fences should be made much more visible – and often are, sometimes with wooden slats, which seems to improve matters.

And that seems to be as far as the discussion goes. I have, myself, a feeling that even all these factors put together are not quite enough to account for the fact that the caper is once again heading – rapidly – for extinction. I think there must be something else going on. I am no geneticist, but I do know that that population of some 20,000 birds derived from two or three reintroductions of, at the most, a couple of hundred birds from Sweden. Since then there has been no new blood; I cannot see that we should expect that a population, coming from such a narrow base, should carry on growing ad infinitum, especially when it belongs to such a temperamental species as the grouse. At the very least, it might become, slowly, less resilient, especially in the face of all the other factors just listed. When we rather blithely reintroduce birds of prey like the red kite and the sea eagle, or the osprey to places like Rutland Water, I simply do not see what harm it could do to try a small-scale reintroduction of caper from another part of Europe, and see what happens. It clearly will not be easy, but surely it is worth a try?

Eleven

ASPECTS OF THE CULTURE

So far, I have referred to many of the larger Highland sporting estates, but there were, of course, a great many small ones
too. When driving around what is now known as Highland
Perthshire, particularly around Strathardle and Glen Shee, I
have been struck by the number of notable houses along the
River Ericht, where each small or medium-sized estate seemed
to manage to have its share of the river and its fishing, some of
the waterside agricultural land for a Home Farm, ornamental
woods and plantations (and often the site for the lodge) on the
steeper glen sides, and a section of the undulating heather-clad
moorland (where the grouse-shooting, on this drier east side
of Scotland, was good) higher up. No doubt, this profusion of
small but prestigious estates derived from their closeness to the
important industrial town of Dundee. The same is true of much
of Argyll, easily reached from Glasgow. Perhaps the major difference here was that the grouse did not do so well; there were
probably more deer, but this, again, may well be when fallow
deer were introduced to the Perthshire hills and glens.

All this building and the complete re-planning of the surrounding lands indicate how extraordinarily popular the
Highland sporting estate had become. I have referred briefly to
the artists whose pictures were hung on the walls of the lodges,
and an indication of how fashionable this all was may be the

fact that the famous, unforgettable image of animal nobility, Sir Edwin Landseer's 'Monarch of the Glen', was commissioned by the Government to hang in the House of Lords.

Writing about the Highlands also had its enthusiastic followers. One wonderful example is *A Summer in Skye* (1865, also published by Birlinn in 1998), in which the author, Alexander Smith, 'a young poet and essayist, who seven years earlier had married a Skye-woman and fell as deeply in love with her island as his Flora, left the noise and bustle of Edinburgh behind to spend six weeks amid the silence of the hills'. As it happens, his wife Flora (who receives fairly scant mention in the book) was the daughter of Charles MacDonald of Ord in Sleat, and I first heard of, and acquired the book, when I lived there. Ord House, that wonderfully situated and dignified laird's house, was Smith's base for his understandably precious holiday. And it makes for wonderful reading if you have some literary stamina:

> *Twice every twenty-four hours the Atlantic tide sets in upon the hallowed shores; twice is the sea withdrawn, leaving spaces of smooth sand on which mermaids, with golden combs, might sleek alluring tresses; and black rocks, heaped with brown dulse and tangle and lovely ocean blooms of purple and orange; and bare islets – marked at full tide by a glimmer of pale green amid the universal sparkle – where most the sea-fowl love to congregate. To these islets on favourable evenings, come the crows and sit in sable parliament; business despatched, they start into air as at a gun and stream away through the sunset to their roosting-place in the Armadale woods.*

The section of shore which Smith is describing there, from the bay of Ord itself, round by the islets to the sea loch of Eishort, is extraordinarily beautiful, and I was extremely fortunate to live there, if only for a few years. The views in all directions from the shores of the Sleat peninsula are truly fine and, being much influenced by the sometimes wild weather of the Hebrides, provide all the drama and romance that any Victorian could wish for. That sense of romance does linger, perhaps more for the visitor than the permanent resident, and I have seen many people fall under its spell.

One woman who has very firmly put the modern Sleat peninsula on the tourist map, through her well-known establishment at nearby Kinloch Lodge, is the famous cook and writer, Claire Macdonald, wife of Godfrey, eighth Lord Macdonald. His full style, 'The Right Honourable Godfrey James Macdonald of Macdonald, 8th Lord Macdonald, Chief of the Name and Arms of Macdonald, High Chief of Clan Donald and 34th hereditary Chief of Clan Donald', although slightly repetitive, would certainly have engaged the romantic fervour of Victorian society, but as I recall there is very little that is Victorian about either Godfrey or Claire, whom I knew a little when I lived close by. One of her books, however, could be described as Victorian in ethos. *Claire Macdonald's Scotland: The Best of Scottish Food and Drink* (Little, Brown & Co, 1990) features beautiful illustrations of Scottish landscapes, old houses and their interiors (complete with fine furniture, ancestral portraits and some sporting pictures), along with one or two kilted proprietors, certainly emphasising the enduring strength of the atmosphere of the sporting estate. Some of the establishments featured, including Inverlochy Castle near Fort William, Ardsheal House in Argyll, and Cringletie House Hotel, Peebles-shire, are truly Victorian houses in the grand manner.

Another lovely and very relevant book is E.P. Harrison's *Scottish Estate Tweeds* (1995) by Johnstons of Elgin, a firm that, like the unique Campbells of Beauly (The Highland Tweed House), catered for the needs of these families and their retainers for a long period, and is still flourishing. *Scottish Estate Tweeds* is much more than the story of a Highland family business; it gives very detailed insights into aspects of the sporting estate. Here is the account of one estate tweed, the Eilanreach:

Eilanreach lies on the Sound of Sleat, on the mainland, just opposite the Isle of Skye (in fact, roughly across the Sound from Kinloch) near Glenelg. It is owned by Lord Dulverton, and was purchased by his father in 1947. The tweed was designed around 1950 by Lord and Lady Dulverton and Sir John Macleod who owned the Cuchulin Handloom Company. Originally the estate was owned by the Baillies of Dochfour, and was rented for a number of years by the Master of Blantyre. The estate was then sold to the Scott family from the Hill of Nigg who in turn sold it to the Dulvertons in 1947. The tweed is unusual in having a bold black and yellow twist for its warp overcheck element.

Although it might be hard to trace all the connections, there is considerable detail here, both of the individual families and their property transactions over the years. It is extraordinary how often the same families crop up – the Dulvertons and Baillies of Dochfour both reappear in several other contexts. Again, it is noteworthy that new tweeds are still being designed and commissioned for some of these sporting estates.

Some of the tweeds are what is known as a simple Shepherd check. This was worn by a child who would eventually become an informal tenant on the Eilanreach Estate (possibly at times something of a thorn in its flesh,) and one of the most-published authors of our time. Gavin Maxwell was an aristocrat, born in 1914, just as our era was about to end in the horrors of the Great War, and very much an inheritor of all the attitudes and trappings of the sporting estate. His great classic of nature writing, the book that influenced a whole generation of lovers of wild country, *Ring of Bright Water* (Longmans, 1960), makes this clear in its first pages:

> There existed during my time at Oxford a curious clique of landed gentry so assertively un-urban that we affected a way of dressing quite unsuited to University life; at all times, for instance, we wore tweed shooting-suits and heavy shooting shoes studded with nails and dull with dubbin, and at our heels trotted spaniels or Labrador retrievers. Some of us were Englishmen, but the majority were Scots or those whose parents were in the habit of renting Highland shootings, and I have no doubt that the cult was akin to my own, for I remember that in the autumn term the rooms of its members were hung with the heads of stags killed during the vac., and there was endless talk of the Highlands.

Gavin Maxwell was a temperamental, tantalising man (whom I wish I had known) with a genius for complicating his own life and causing havoc in the lives of others, as well as for describing the fascination and beauty of the landscape which he inhabited, that of the Western Highlands. The setting of *Ring of Bright Water* he called Camusfearna, The Bay of the Alders, but anyone who knew the West Coast was able to identify its approximate location by the cover of the hardback, with its splendid photograph of the very distinct profile of Ben Sgriol, fronted by the tranquil waters of Loch Hourn. He records that the owner of the estate surrounding his isolated cottage was of an experimental turn-of-mind, keen at one time on raising cattle that hung around the cottage and the shore, and latterly on forestry. This had, in its turn, become very fashionable as a form of land-use, deriving partly from the experience of creating the splendid and beautiful policy-woodlands to which I have already referred. Sadly, forestry was, and is, much more about the hope of making money out of the countryside, and rarely about beauty. The trees that were found to grow well and quickly in the Scottish Highlands have often been planted all over the country in regimented blocks, with very little thought, if any, about the look of the countryside so transformed.

Government policy has not always been very helpful in this context; there have long been grants to encourage forestry, but one Government in particular decided to abolish grants for management, which crucially included the thinning of trees that need to be planted close together to help provide mutual shelter in their early years. Without later thinning, the plantations become impossibly dense and dark, the trees tall, spindly and covered in a prickly mess of dead branches, and almost no light reaches the naked ground. There are plantations like this all over the Highlands, and they have to be clear-felled, as it is impossible to select and remove individual trees.

I have visited Camusfearna (or Sandaig, its proper name) on several occasions, and I made notes immediately after one walk there in the winter. I had been lecturing in Glenelg the evening before, staying with a young and wonderfully bilingual family overnight. After breakfast, as it was a beautiful day, I decided to look around before returning home. Here are the notes I made on my return, only slightly augmented.

Today woke to a glorious winter morning, and leaving the lovely family with whom I had been staying, I drove south past Eileanreach, an attractive lodge, and through the overwhelming conifers, past Upper Sandaig – dwarfed by them – and turning towards Loch Hourn, through the hell that is clear-fell. What a bloody mess. Then (apt lesson) past an attractive hanging natural wood of oak, birch and holly, down to Arnisdale and Corran. The huge, snowy hills were largely wrapped in cloud (certainly all the high tops) but the views across the Sound to Sleat were good. Beyond, a glimpse of a snowy summit of Rum, and part of a Cuillin, shining out through a gap in the heavy cloud like a distant Himalayan peak.

I turned, drove back, parked at the Forestry gate above Sandaig, and walked down the track through dark, uninspiring, mature conifers; eventually, steeply down a rough track by the old telephone posts, descending to the flatter ground by the sea. I walked on the north side of the burn, still fringed with alders, and out to the rough headland that overlooks the group of small, craggy islets, the shining sands, and the Sandaig light. I sat for a good while and drank it all in.

The islets here remind me of those beyond Ord; the seaweed wet and dark, the dry rock bright in the cold, clear light, the heather a rich brown with the russet of dead bracken, the sand almost white, and the water a subtle, translucent silk, all colours from ivory to deep blue-green.

There were pairs of mergansers, the males alert for interlopers, and lots of herons, skinny silhouettes against the bright sea. There was a small group of eiders, the females as dark as the winter heather, the males black-and-white in the distance, subtle with soft peach and sage-green through the glasses. And that woodwind-music call...

Then across the burn, very low at the moment, and along the shore to the stones for Edal and Gavin, where I stopped and pondered for a while. Also paid my homage at the waterfall, now rather hemmed-in by the conifers, reduced in stature, diminished in flow, unblessed by the white of young bodies cooling-off on a summer day...

Eventually retreated up the hill; pine marten skat on the track. Huge grey-white hills loomed from Ratagan on my way home in a complex half-circle that took me back to Sleat, halfway almost to Eigg, which I had seen from Sandaig. A quiet evening, thinking about the literary and emotional legacy of this unlikely product of the sporting culture...

oto: © Paul Wordingham

Above: Dunrobin Castle, Sutherland.

PHOTO: © ROB FARROW

Above: Kinloch Castle, Isle of Rum.

Opposite, above: Balmoral Castle, Royal Deeside.

Opposite, below: Ornamental railing, Ardross Castle, Ross-shire.

Below: Balfour Castle, Shapinsay.

PHOTO: © GRAHAM LAIRD

PHOTO: © ROBIN NOBLE

Left: Cock capercaillie.

Opposite, above: Red stag during the rut.

PHOTO: © RICHARD BARTZ

Opposite, below: Abandoned cottage, East Sutherland.

Below: Old Scots pines, Ryvoan, Speyside.

Opposite, above: Native trees, Glencanisp, Assynt.

Opposite, below: Suspension bridge over the River Oykell, Sutherland.

Below: Regenerating pinewood, Rothiemurchus.

Bottom: Victorian landscape, Strath Rusdale, Ross-shire.

PHOTO: © PHIL CHAMPION

Above: Ossian's Hall, the Hermitage, Dunkeld.

Below: Woodland glade, Trumland, Rousay.

PHOTO: © COLIN PARK

Twelve

NEW LANDSCAPES

All the construction, earth-moving, tree-planting and so on that took place on the Victorian estates was extremely labour-intensive and, somewhat ironically, the Highlands, post-Clearances, seem not to have had an adequate workforce for some of these tasks; labourers and craftsmen were often brought in from elsewhere. In Ardross, the village now called Dublin records the presence of Irish navvies involved in Dyson Perrin's great work. Even after the construction phase, these estates employed a considerable number, and small estate villages like the Crask of Aigas show where they all lived. Wealthier landowners built larger villages like Beauly, and some are very attractive to look at and almost small towns: Inveraray in Argyll, close by the Duke's new castle, or Grantown-on-Spey.

Rivers were not immune from the mania for 'improvement'; we have seen that encouraging considerable numbers of salmon was important to the new sporting lairds. A few, like Lord Salisbury, failed to achieve much, but all over the Highlands you may find the smallest of lochs provided with a dam and sluice, both enlarging the area of the loch and permitting you to let a small spate down it, in order to bring the salmon or sea trout up to spawn, or be caught on the way.

Larger rivers were much altered, too; there is a natural tendency for short, fast Highland rivers to develop long, shallow rapids, but fish do not lie long in such places, and the fishing of them itself is difficult. In such places, the natural flow of water was often much modified by the construction of croys, low stone piers reaching into the middle of the current from either bank. These, acting almost like a dam, heightened the water, creating nice calm pools, with a short, fast current between them, through which the fish might easily pass. Many rivers show such extensive modification; the Star Pool on the River Inver is the one I know best, having walked beside it since childhood, but the much smaller pools beside my cottage retained vestigial croys, which I enjoyed rebuilding on midge-free summer days. The Oykell, a major Sutherland river, has a number of them, probably older than the ones on the Inver, and it boasts, too, a fine pedestrian suspension bridge, built to allow anglers to cross from one bank to another.

Following the new trends in agriculture at the time, riverside fields were drained, fertilised and reseeded or cropped according to the modern idea of rotations. New trees were planted, either in shelter-belts, plantations or the policies around the Big House, and artificially high numbers of grouse or deer (or both) were being encouraged on the moor and open hill. This was becoming an entirely managed landscape, and with it came compartmentalisation: slowly the North was criss-crossed with fences, which often became significant barriers as the number of deer grew.

Methods of management progressively heightened the differences between the compartments of these 'new' landscapes. Now that winter-feed was much more available than it had been in the past, larger numbers of stock were retained than before, and as the sheiling-system (by which the summer growth on the higher hills was exploited, while, crucially, the vegetation around the permanent settlements was given a rest) was abolished, the impact of the livestock was all the greater. It is true that if the estate ran sheep, those animals would be very carefully and precisely herded on a daily basis, but their numbers were significantly higher than before the Clearances. In any case, that active shepherding has slowly declined through time, and now almost disappeared totally. In Assynt, it was still being practised when I was young, but has now totally gone – as have, of course, many of the sheep.

The numbers of deer were being increased in different ways, with winter-feeding to avoid the normal heavy mortality of the season, and the importing of park stock from England to 'improve' the breed; this simply meant to make them larger, with bigger antlers for your ballroom. If sheep numbers did decline in any one area, the deer would probably move into the vacated lands, and, all in all, grazing throughout the Highlands and Islands must have constantly increased throughout our period. The impact of this grazing varied, of course, throughout the year. In spring, for example, the deer are often simply starving, but the grass may well not have started to grow significantly. What does appear at this time is the brilliant, fresh green of regenerating birch, which happens most effectively in dry heather ground alongside a mature stand of trees, and against the deep brown of the heather the new leaves are all too obvious – and do not last long. Our native trees prefer to regenerate in the open rather than in the shade of their parents, but constant grazing around small groups of birch simply spells death to the next generation, and, ultimately, the end of the wood. Less obvious, perhaps, than the effect of heavy grazing on seedling trees, is the effect on heather, which is ultimately suppressed. It is not always recognised that heather is very nutritious, and being somewhat evergreen in character (as a close inspection in the dead of winter will reveal), it is much eaten during that season and the spring. While heather reacts well to burning, it simply cannot cope with heavy grazing, which will finish it.

Even after many years in the Highlands, I only recognised the extent of this effect in very recent years. I must have driven via Cluanie Inn and down Glen Shiel for over forty years, during which time I had always assumed that the grassy nature of the big hills here was due either to the presence of some particular minerals in the parent rocks, or to the very heavy rainfall of the area, or both. But I was completely wrong; some small exclosures, erected several years ago, are now a noticeably different colour from their surroundings. The heather, long suppressed by very heavy grazing, is returning.

Worse, perhaps, even than heavy grazing, is the trampling of wet ground by thousands of sharp hooves, which destroys the mosses that form the surface of a healthy bog and help to prevent erosion. Whether the extensive and fearsome black peat-hags found in some places are natural in origin or not is still debated, but there is little reason to doubt that trampling makes the problem much worse.

I mentioned heather-burning, or 'muirburn', above; although it had certainly been used as a management tool for many centuries, perhaps even for thousands of years, there can be little doubt that it increased significantly during our era, as the creation and maintenance of the grouse moor became so important. Heather is (although many people may not know it) a woody shrub, which can grow quite easily to three or four feet in height. It is highly combustible, but responds to burning with tender young shoots, which are in themselves very nutritious, and within a couple of years also tend to flower prolifically, attracting insects. The purpose of burning, as part of grouse moor management, is to create a mosaic of patches of heather of different ages and heights, with the short young shoots and flowering plants providing food, and the longer providing shelter for birds to hide from the weather or predators. The resultant characteristic patterning of the land is very noticeable, and is commonly seen in many places particularly in the Eastern Highlands.

Immediately after burning, and before the heather has started to re-appear, there tends to be a quick regrowth of some of the coarser moorland grasses, especially *Molinia*, and because the fresh shoots are relatively tender, they are eaten both by sheep and deer, which meant that the habit of burning was taken up or continued by shepherds and crofters. We have ended up with some sort of 'east-west' split in the practice and effect of muirburn. As mentioned, the burning in the Eastern Highlands is mostly on grouse moors, and is intense and controlled (although some fires do get out of hand). This certainly results in some wonderful expanses of blooming heather (the Scotland of the shortbread-tin), but it tends very much to be a monoculture of heather, devoid of much else. Under such regular burning, there is little chance that any seedling trees will escape, so woodland regeneration is unlikely, made all the rarer by the fact that the common tree of these areas is the Scots pine, which is, along with the juniper (with which it often grows), also extremely combustible. Unlike heather, however, both pine and juniper die when burnt. The ultimate effect is to increase the compartmentalised aspect of the new Highlands: if you have managed grouse moor, you will not have trees. The effect is often further exacerbated by grazing subsequent to the burning; in Perthshire and Angus I have seen many blackface sheep and three species of deer together, closely grazing the burnt areas. Small wonder that during the course of an informal survey, I concluded that the surrounding moorland was among the most limited in flowering species that I had ever seen, despite its relatively dry nature.

In contrast, in the much wetter West, burning has long been less frequent and far less controlled, with much larger patches being burnt, and the occasional catastrophic event when the fire gets totally out of control and extends over a huge area. At times, these wildfires have been seen as a possible danger to human life; there have certainly been threats to property, and some horrific occasions when the very compartmentalised nature of the modern Highlands, divided by high fences, has led to the trapping and death of some deer. New woodland plantings and some areas of regeneration have also suffered badly. The immediate aftermath of a major burn is undeniably ghastly, and after each one there are inevitably calls for the practice to be banned, or greater measures of control to be put in place. All this, understandably, obscures one critical fact, which is that without regular burning there will inevitably be a build-up of combustible material (apart from the heather itself, dry *Molinia* burns frighteningly well), which will one day catch fire – perhaps through a lightning strike, but more likely because of a carelessly-extinguished cigarette (in fact, one of the major causes of catastrophic fires in Assynt and Coigach in recent decades has been tidy gardeners having bonfires). There is just not the labour force in such crofting areas to burn on a controlled basis, and the enormous surrounding acreages of land are consequently at risk. The problem remains intractable, if intermittent.

One of the problems of such fires is that the peat or peaty soil under the heather may itself catch fire and smoulder for days. Where such soil is thin – on stony hillsides or around crags, for instance – it becomes friable and erodes very quickly, increasing the inherent stoniness of much of the Highlands and Islands. Such places should just never be burnt, but often, right across the country, this is ignored. The visible effects of a severe burn may remain obvious for years, even decades. I can still point out where a serious heath-fire in the Orcadian island of Hoy, which occurred in the 1980s, actually terminated. It was, incidentally, one of two critical factors that helped drive golden eagles from these splendid hills.

When I was living in Assynt, I did a careful study of the effects of muirburn in the region, and concluded that the occasional burning of dry areas, perhaps once in ten years or more (it was hard to be precise about the timing), was beneficial to biodiversity – in other words, to the presence of flowering plants. The first few years after a burn showed a great increase in the numbers of tormentil, eyebright, milkwort, some vetches and hawkweeds, the lovely slender St John's wort and some orchids. As the heather slowly grew and shaded them out, they of course declined, until they were only just present – until the next burn. Birch saplings quite often survived scorching in a fire, although they might have to spring again from the base, and a fire running through a mature wood normally did little harm in the longer run. Overall, in the forty or so years for which I had photographic evidence for the changes in the vegetation around Drumbeg, the wooded nature of the area had slowly increased, despite the frequency of burning. Some species were, however, badly affected: the amount of juniper present in any one area could be used to reveal how much burning that place had experienced over the years – much of Assynt has very little.

It is clear, but often overlooked, that lichens (which may grow extraordinarily slowly) are likely to be destroyed during a fire, certainly during repeated fires.

I was not so clear about the effects on damper areas – which is much of Assynt. If they were wet on the surface, as in many years, any fire just ran lightly over them, taking out the few bits of heather and the odd patch of dry *Molinia* without, it seemed, doing much fundamental damage. But some years we might often have a long spell of cold but desiccating easterly winds, which dried out and blanched the normally colourful sphagnum mosses on the surface of the bog. These then burnt, and needed some years to recover visibly; sadly, it would take a more precise botanical eye than mine to ascertain whether there was a significant reduction in the number of moss species. The real, subsequent damage was often, again, the result of trampling which, if serious, would destroy the depleted vegetation and begin the erosion of the wet peat beneath.

One conclusion my woodland survey work over several years did make absolutely clear was that, within crofting areas in sheltered places close to the coast, there has often been significant new growth of birch woods on land that we know was cultivated before the Clearances. A few other tree species have also seen this regeneration: rowan, alder and some willows, with shrubs like blackthorn and hazel enjoying the stony banks of new roads. What evidence we have suggests that this growth started quite soon after the Clearances, and had what might be called 'a final fling' during and after the 1950s. Birch regeneration may still be seen, moving in dense bands across the lower ground, sometimes despite the undoubted presence of sheep and happy pyromaniacs. Holly, again nutritious and much eaten in hard winters, has to fight to get away, but sometimes succeeds, while oak, wych elm and bird cherry seem to struggle. We do not yet fully understand the dynamics of native West Coast woodland, but there still remains a surprising amount of it, which is something. What is not quite so clear is how it will fare in future; the ever-increasing numbers of deer, especially red deer, put it all in question. The compartments in our new landscapes are far from watertight; the deer have escaped from the confines of the deer forests, and are now everywhere.

Thirteen

A WALK IN COIGACH

When my father ceased making whisky, my parents retired to a house that had latterly been their holiday-home, at the landward end of the Coigach peninsula – quite close, ironically, to the ruins of an illicit still. Old photographs showed that it had originally been, like Glenleraig, a very modest shepherd's cottage, which had grown over the years. They made it into a lovely place, with a nice garden (rhododendrons and azaleas, of course!) running down to a tumbling burn, and an excellent view over a wide, flat valley to the elegant ridges of An Teallach. At its back were ranged the peaks of Coigach, the spires and walls of Ben More looking particularly splendid, although it must be confessed that they did hold the cloud and the rain in the long winter months.

I have known the place for many years and done several walks from there. One of my all-time favourites takes you into the hills at the back of the house, into the fastnesses of the Drumrunie Forest, from which sheep have long since been banished. The best way to get there is to take the single-track road west towards the sea, the islands and Achilitibuie. Within a few miles you skirt the lower crags of Cul Beag and reach the head of the long, hill-girt Loch Lurgainn, on which my father had a boat, and from which we had taken the occasional sea trout. At this point, there rises ahead of you what is probably the most astonishing little mountain in all Britain, the spectacularly eroding sandstone pinnacles of Stac Pollaidh. Before you reach it, and just before another lonely roadside cottage, there is just about enough space to park by the verge and set off for the day.

The path, for once not too rough, rises up through the remnants of a plantation of Scots pine, but enough trees have died for it to be quite spacious and pleasant, an asset to the scenery, and it is with a high heart that you continue up the hill. Quite soon, the path begins to level out, you reach a lochan and a great, purple boulder of sandstone, and pause to enjoy the open views ahead. Northwards are the great hills: Cul Mor, Suilven and my own Quinag, like the prows of great ships heading westwards over the wet confusion of the lower land. As you continue along the easy path, you start to see into the ground ahead of you; between the peak of Cul Beag, which is rearing up on your right, and the mass of Cul Mor, there is a complex valley of lochs and woods, into which you have to descend.

Given the names of these twin hills of Coigach, a brief, explanatory digression may be permitted here, as they are somewhat intriguing. Most lovers of the Highlands will know that *mor* means 'big', and *beag* means 'little' – they're often Anglicised to 'more' and 'beg'. The *cul* element is one of a number of Gaelic words that are shared with French, and although many prim dictionaries will provide you with 'back', it is not exactly your 'back' that is covered by your 'culottes'. The resemblance may not leap to the eye, especially in the case of the lower hill but, like it or not, these must be the 'buttock' hills, perhaps so named from the twin peaks of Cul Mor, which are conspicuous from other directions.

If you decide to do the roughly circular walk in a clockwise direction, you leave the main path a little while after the highest point, descending gently towards an isthmus between the two nearest lochs. The larger loch, the right hand one, has a couple of inviting sandy beaches, just where you cross two small, peaty burns. The sand is an exquisite pink, derived from the surrounding purple sandstone, and it is hard to resist the temptation to swim on a warm day, although it is very shallow and necessary to wade far out to find an adequate depth. Fortunately, the bank behind the beach is low and not covered with trees, so there is nearly always a breeze to help keep the dreaded midges at bay. The surroundings are splendid, but it is the great, terraced side of Cul Mor, its lower part wooded, that draws the eye. In the spring, there are cuckoos here, willow warblers calling from every bush, and greenshank piping as they fly overhead, so as you scan the imposing hills you are conscious all the time of their ancient music.

It is an easy, if at times boggy, walk along the isthmus; some sandstone slabs provide an occasional dry section. The path leads across a low-lying area towards the head of a very big loch now appearing on the left; this is Sionascaig, home of black-throated divers, whose exultant, ululating call is occasionally heard. Next, one meets the outflow from the system of lochs on the right – this is a complicated place! – and if it has been raining for the last few days, you may experience some difficulty in crossing dry-shod. (There was once a bridge here, and a few maps still mark it, but it disappeared long ago.) Once that is achieved, the way is easier for quite some time.

Turning right, heading upstream, the long, rather depleted wood with a complicated Gaelic name, which means 'the wood of the sandy loch' (a fair description), will be above you, and you will rapidly realise that this low-lying ground was once very definitely inhabited. And it is easy to see why. It is most attractive, largely sheltered, sunny, fairly well-drained, and still quite green; some structures remain. Some old trees overhang the meandering burn, and everywhere can be heard the sound of water; there are several falls among the high rocks that make this place so remarkable. It is precisely from so many inland places like this that folk were being cleared throughout the long period during which the big sporting estates were being established. The people who lived in this sheltered glen may well have been evicted to the already crowded coast, given a small patch of much poorer and totally unsheltered land, and told to take up fishing. This may well have been a softer option than taking ship to Canada, but it was hardly easy.

When I was last in this place, it was in connection with a woodland survey I was carrying out for the owners, the community body known as the Assynt Foundation. It was not long since a major heath-fire had swept from the western end of Cul Mor across a large area, around the shore of Loch Sionascaig, almost to the sea. At that stage, it was all too easy to work out exactly where the fire had rampaged as the area affected appeared much rockier than untouched places, with only a thin green staining from the new growth of hill grasses. It was, I think, never known how the fire started, but guessed to be caused by some folk wild-camping in this beautiful place. If so, a few moments' carelessness certainly ravaged an enormous area.

While walking this way on another occasion with a few friends, we were slowly gaining height above the long burn, and tending to spend most of our time looking for eagles high in the sky, when I happened to look down at a broad, shallow section of the water below us. There, in profile, was an otter, which we followed for a while as it made its way slowly upstream, investigating banks, guddling around in shallow pools, completely unaware of our presence until it disappeared among rocks, where, presumably, it had its holt.

Unsurprisingly, this burn comes from another piece of water: Lochan Dearg, the 'small, red loch', presumably again from its shallow, sandy nature. This is as far up the valley as we normally would go, and turning, the way lies through another, extremely sad, wood; just a few dying trees. The whole area being explored, from the hills of Cul Beag and Cul Mor to the distant sea, was once the Inverpolly National Nature Reserve, one of the flagships for nature conservation in Scotland – or that was the intention. Unlike other NNRs, such as Beinn Eighe in Torridon, Inverpolly was never owned by the Nature Conservancy Council or its successor, SNH. It depended on management agreements with the relevant estates, which were, ultimately, not strong enough to protect the nature-conservation interest in this diverse and wonderful area. To put it bluntly, the real problem was the sporting interest, the deer, and as the conservation of nature could not be held to be paramount, the NNR was 'de-notified' – in other words, abandoned. To be fair, there are still significant designations in place, but in terms of public relations it was a disaster, suggesting that our protection of the natural heritage was – and is – rather weak.

Further along the walk, above the next, bigger loch, there are again problems of moribund woodland, where past attempts to remedy the situation have achieved little. The clear problem is that once you lose a natural, hill-side woodland within a deer forest, it is impossible to reinstate it without very obvious, heavy-handed measures including fencing and planting. This wood is constrained by the high, rocky hillside above and a flat shelf of sodden bog below, so is additionally hampered by having little room for manoeuvre and a seed-source that may be just too far away. Only desperate measures will make any difference here, and no one has had the courage to undertake them – yet.

When the inhabitants of this wonderful valley were removed to the coast, they may well have been shunted through a few different locations, before finally being given some security of tenure. As I have made clear, there was not much room on the coast, and the ground was poorer and blasted by salt winds. It has always seemed to me a rather sad irony, although understandable, that the first 'official' crofters followed the example of the landowners who had dispossessed them, and turned to the sheep to sustain them. Just as some of the first sheep-farmers put far too many on the land, and rapidly had to reduce their flocks, so some of the crofters discovered that the exposed, coastal headlands were nothing like as fertile as the inland glens they had known, and so they, the sheep, and the land suffered accordingly. The crofts were supposed each to have a small patch of arable land, but it was often wet (fields of useless rushes are a common sight today), while some common grazings are as bleak and poor a piece of ground as you may find anywhere. Many such areas slowly became depopulated until the fashion for holiday-cottages and retirement homes saw the empty houses purchased and renovated.

Such areas had long been without significant woodland, and peat, of which there was normally plenty, was cut for fuel. The lines of old peat-banks may often be seen in the flatter parts, particularly in the Islands, and on the West Coast. In this domestic cutting, done of course by hand, the vegetated surface of the area being cut in any particular year was removed and chucked down to cover the bare zone that had been cut during the previous season. This means, at least, that little ecological damage is done; in fact, as the pieces of turf are usually replaced somewhat haphazardly, they do not fit together perfectly and edges are often left raised, resting on another piece of the somewhat soggy jigsaw. This allows rather better drainage, the heather grows longer, and small mammals and birds enjoy this more favourable habitat. The hills of Mainland Orkney have extensive peat-cuttings and the lines so created may be seen at quite a distance. When hen harriers were still common in Orkney, I used to watch them flying low along the strips of deeper heather in search of voles and meadow-pipits.

Of course, not all crofting areas were as bleak as some of the headlands of Wester Ross, and many parts of Skye, for instance, look comparatively fertile, populated and prosperous – which they are. The croft-houses had to be built by the actual crofter and, in contrast with the close-huddled blackhouses I had seen in Tusdale, these are separate, each built within their own croft land. Initially only of one storey, with a skylight in the loft like my cottage in Glenleraig, they gradually acquired substantial upper floors, often with dormer windows, a style that remains common today. When I was young, few of them had gardens, but throughout the 1970s the fashion for planting windbreaks of conifers took hold. Just as in the landlord's plantations, they were planted close together in order to provide mutual shelter when young and delicate, but they were never thinned and grew far too tall, towering over many of the houses and blocking most of the sunlight. As I write, I am informed by my brother that the West Coast is experiencing regular and violent gales; no doubt the remaining such trees, those which exasperated owners have not yet felled, are being toppled by the forces of nature. The very real trouble with experiments in land management, and particularly in forestry, is that they take a long time to assess, and mistakes – they so often are mistakes – remain glaringly obvious for decades afterwards.

Fourteen

GAMEKEEPING AND OTHER IMPACTS

We have seen that the most desired quarry for our Victorian sportsmen were the red deer, salmon and grouse. But there were others. For instance, other species of deer: roe, fallow and sika where introduced or, now, in places to which they have made their own way. As muntjac have been seen in the Highlands in recent years, they will presumably be added to the list, to join wild (or long-term feral) goats and, soon perhaps, feral boar. Hares, brown and blue, complete the mammals; rabbits were simply a pest and shot at will.

The salmon were accompanied by their close relatives, the sea trout – which often put up a splendid fight – and brown trout. Some lochs contained Arctic char (rare and desirable) and pike, rather less desirable, were introduced into a few river systems. Eels, which were certainly plentiful, were not on the desirable list, and were extremely difficult to kill, making a dreadful mess of line and cast in the process.

Of the birds, capercaillie, the great grouse of the forest, have already been mentioned in some detail; ptarmigan on the high tops were, like the woodcock, shot by the few sportsmen who ventured north in the winter months. Black grouse and grey partridge were still quite common, while only a few Highland estates introduced pheasant or red-legged partridge; these are very much a recent phenomenon. Quail, I think, were rare. Several species of duck were shot, and geese, if there were any around (rarer then than now, as it happens). Woodcock belong to the waders, and of that family, snipe are still shot, more surely because of the fact that they are a very challenging shot than because of their actual meat. Dotterel, golden and green plover (the lapwing), and curlew once featured, but no longer do. Wood pigeons were rather like rabbits, but quite a test of the sportsman's ability.

Quantities mattered a lot to these sportsmen. The numbers actually killed were carefully recorded in countless gamebooks, along with weights of fish or the number of points on a stag's antlers, and the conditions of the day. The men whose responsibility it was to produce the greatest possible numbers of all these quarry species, and who now became hugely significant figures throughout the Highlands and Islands, were the gamekeepers. Throughout our period, up until the outbreak of conflict in 1914, the gamekeepers waged a constant war against any species regarded as vermin, any creature that might reduce the number or condition of the precious game.

I have earlier mentioned two occasional papers produced by SNH, and I now quote them again in detail. Referring to precisely this war against vermin, Chris Smout, in 'The Highlands and the Roots of Green Consciousness, 1750–1990', writes:

With the game came gamekeepers, and technology in due course supplied them with deadly weapons against predators, the cartridge-loading shotgun and the steel gin trap. Early game books are full of details of the destruction of birds of prey on a scale which has occasionally tested credulity: for example, in five Aberdeenshire parishes around Braemar, 70 eagles, and 2520 hawks and kites are said to have been killed between 1776 and 1786; on the Sutherland estates of Langwell and Sandside, 295 adult eagles were destroyed between 1819 and 1826; on a single estate south of the Forests of Gaick and Glen Feshie, well over 1000 kestrels and buzzards, 275 kites, 98 peregrine falcons, 78 merlins, 92 hen harriers, 63 goshawks, 106 owls, 18 ospreys, 42 eagles and sundry other hawks, in only three years, 1837– 1840. To take a Lowland example, 310 hen harriers were killed on one Ayrshire estate in four years of the 19th century.

The other Occasional Paper, 'Ill Fares the Land', is by John Lister-Kaye, founder of Aigas Field Centre, where I still often teach. This topic comes up regularly, and I refer to the following paragraphs, reading them aloud (you might care to do so yourself; it allows the content to be more fully understood). It concerns the estate of:

Glengarry, until recently the property of the chief of the clan of Macdonald... [which] was sold in 1840 to Lord Ward for £91,000 (over £2.5 million today/1994). It abounds in game... but like most estates... has also been subject to the ravages of vermin. From the lordly eagle down to the stot and weasel, those destructive denizens of the wood and wild find ample room for exertion amid the vast and unploughed recesses of the Highland glens and forests...Annoyed by the loss of game, this gentleman engaged numerous gamekeepers... and awarding prizes of £3 to £5 to each of those who should prove the most successful... The keepers pursued the slaughter with undeviating rigour and attention.

The following is the list of vermin destroyed at Glengarry, from Whitsunday 1837 to Whitsunday 1840: 11 foxes; 108 wildcats; 246 martin cats; 106 polecats; 301 stots and wea-sels; 67 badgers; 48 otters; 78 house cats going wild; 27 white-tailed sea eagles; 15 golden eagles; 18 osprey or fishing-eagles; 98 blue hawks or peregrine falcons; 7 orange-legged falcons; 11 hobby hawks; 275 kites, commonly called salmon-tailed gledes; 5 marsh harriers or yellow-legged hawks; 63 goshawks; 285 common buzzards; 371 rough-legged buzzards; 3 honey buzzards; 462 kestrils or red-hawks; 78 merlin hawks; 83 hen harriers or ring-tailed hawks; 6 jer-falcon or toe-feathered hawks; 9 ash-coloured or long blue-tailed hawks; 1431 hooded or carrion crows; 475 ravens; 35 horned owls; 71 common fern owls; 3 golden owls; and 3 magpies.

This amounts to over 4,000 'head of vermin', killed on one Highland estate in three years.

The implications of this overwhelming evidence are critically important, but before we consider them, it is worth referring to the judgment of Chris Smout and John Lister–Kaye, as to how credible these totals are.

Chris Smout: 'My own view is that there is so much of this evidence from such varied sources that it cannot be disregarded in total, although some details of species identification may be wrong.'

John Lister–Kaye: 'Game-book evidence is so widespread for this period that, even if some records are exaggerated… it is clear that all estates held a fervent commitment to the extirpation of all predatory wildlife.'

Their conclusions are clear, and of the highest importance.

Chris Smout: 'The destruction of the birds of prey on this scale was itself a major modification of the natural world. Small mammal predators suffered at least as badly…

'At least as significant as the fact of their destruction is what the former volume of predators reveals about the volume of prey species in the Highlands – voles, mice, hares, small birds and so on. They clearly no longer exist at anything like the densities necessary to support such numbers of predators…'

John Lister–Kaye (quoting Chris Smout): 'To anyone who

works in the Highland hills this academic caution is unjustified. The evidence is stark... The scientific description for uplands is "species poor". For many Highland hills, "species absent" might be more accurate.'

I should make it clear that I see no credible alternative to these conclusions, formed after careful consideration by these two eminent men. For what it is worth, I should perhaps record that I share them. More importantly, I remain convinced that completely inadequate attention has been paid to them, even by those most closely involved in such matters.

What, then, are the implications of all this? What were the Highlands like then, what was Glengarry like in 1837? Whole theses could perhaps be written on the information quoted so far in this single chapter, but I shall try to stick to the most significant issues.

In another book, *Nature Contested* (Edinburgh University Press, 2000), Chris Smout provides brief, anecdotal answers to these fundamental questions. After a section devoted to the most extraordinary numbers of dotterel shot on migration during the 18th and early 19th centuries ('Many hundreds were still shot around 1850'), he quotes Thomas Pennant, travelling in Upper Deeside in the 1760s, who described the zone above the pine woods in terms that recall the first travellers to the American west:

The whole tract abounds with game: the stags at this time were ranging in the mountains, but the little roebucks were perpetu- ally bounding before us; and the black game often sprung under our feet. The tops of hills swarmed with grous and ptarmigans. Green plovers, whimbrels and snowflecks breed here.

And so on. A century later, on the other side of Scotland, in Gairloch, Osgood MacKenzie (of Inverewe Gardens) quoted his game-book for 1868:

My total for that year was 1,314 grouse, 33 blackgame, 49
partridges, 110 golden plover, 35 wild ducks, 53 snipe, 91
rock-pigeons, 184 hares, without mentioning geese, teal, ptar-
migan, and roe, etc., a total of 1900 head. In other seasons I
got sometimes as many as 96 partridges, 106 snipe, and 95
woodcock. Now [1921], so many of these good beasts and birds
are either quite extinct or on the verge of becoming so.

Even family anecdotes, half-lost, reinforce this picture of
plenty. I remember an account my grandmother, born in 1896,
had from her grandfather, whom she had known well and who
lived on the West Coast through this period. He had counted
nineteen ospreys on a trip from Glengarry to Loch Hourn. If,
as I commented in my first chapter, the outline of the beloved
hills remains the same, the overall environment is hugely transformed, almost indescribably the poorer.

It is absolutely clear from all this that the Highlands of only
200 years ago supported a wildlife that was both far more numerous and diverse than it is now. Given the data from Glengarry,
I imagine that a competent, thorough, patient and, above all,
statistically minded naturalist (most certainly not me!) could produce a reasonable environmental model showing, at the least, the
type and volume of prey species that would be required to support that volume of predators. And from that, it should again be
possible to provide some sort of vegetation model, an idea of the
natural environment required to support the implied populations
of prey species... small mammals and birds, but also, of course,
the very game that the keepers were/are trying to protect: the
grouse and plovers, also the hares, particularly in this case the
mountain hares. Has no one tried this? Has SNH, the body that
produced the two Occasional Papers on such a critical matter,
not done this work? It is hard to see how any fundamental deci-
sions about Highland land-use could ever be taken without some

attempt to establish what this environment was actually like.

In the presumed absence of such important, if theoretical, work, we must consider what we know of Glengarry in the relevant period. (Again, there is huge potential for serious work here; this will of necessity be both brief and rather superficial.)

There is no reason to suppose that Glengarry, at this or any other period, was some sort of untouched Highland Eden. In fact, the Cheviot sheep had been introduced there in 1782, over fifty years before, and had presumably flourished, as it was introduced to Caithness ten years later by Sir John Sinclair of Ulbster, and then, of course, all over the Highlands. The mixture of predatory bird species shot suggests a mixed habitat to me, rather than any sort of woodland paradise, and although they provide information for an earlier period (1747–55), the relevant Roy maps seem only to show woodland on the southern side of the river, both below and above the loch. Although it must be clear that almost every type of habitat was richer, I am left with the feeling that the moorland is most relevant here, and this is a subject which Chris Smout goes on to consider in *Nature Contested*. Indeed, the rest of the chapter that I have already quoted is mostly concerned with declining productivity in the moorlands, using detailed figures for numbers of grouse shot on the Buccleuch Estate of Drumlanrig since 1834. Figures are available for red grouse and black, but to my eyes, they reveal a pattern rather similar to that discussed earlier for the capercaillie. They start at quite a low level from 1834–50, with fewer than 1,000 red grouse shot on Drumlanrig and Sanquhar, rising to the extraordinary figure of 'almost 15,000 on the eve of the First World War'. This enormous increase must be at least partly the result of the unceasing war against predators, which lasted until many keepers went to fight, so a subsequent decline is only to be expected, and is certainly confirmed by the figures. The questions really are whether this sheds much light on declining moorland productivity, or whether some genetic factor, common to all our grouse species, is also involved. This is not an easy problem to disentangle, and the worry remains as to how far you may extrapolate the effect of external factors, from the figures of numbers killed. What if they simply shot too many one year? Or several years running?

At this point, it is worth listing the factors of which we may be reasonably confident.

Another of Chris Smout's books, *Scotland since Prehistory: Natural Change and Human Impact* (Scottish Cultural Press, 1993), first alerted me to the probable effects of the regular eruptions of the Icelandic volcano Hekla on the vegetation of the Scottish Highlands and Islands. The explosions at Chernobyl, and the more recent widespread dispersal of volcanic ash (which caused much disruption of flights) from another such volcano have, I imagine, accustomed most readers to the idea of the rapid dispersal of the outpourings from such eruptions over wide areas, and this is in any case confirmed by the presence of volcanic ash in soil sequences from archaeological excavation. The cloud cover caused by such events has a significant, if short-term, effect on climate, but there may be other effects as well. Hekla's eruptions produce fluorine, for instance, which poisons sheep (and presumably other herbivores), so I postulate that mild doses might not exactly benefit hares, for instance, living on affected Scottish moorlands. That is speculative, but the regular eruptions of Hekla during and after our period are not: they occurred in 1766–68, 1845–46, 1878, 1913, 1947–48, 1970, 1980–81, 1991 and 2000.

The effects of acid rain are not speculative either, but well understood. What appears to be forgotten is when they may *first*, un-noticed or unrecognised, have begun to affect the British Isles, particularly the more acid north and west. The Industrial Revolution is normally assumed to have begun around 1750, and was certainly well underway by the time, a century later, our new sporting lairds, many of whose fortunes derived from that same Revolution, arrived in the Highlands. As industrial pollution began noticeably to affect localities immediately around the plants where it was produced, higher chimneys were simply built, with the effect of exporting the pollution to remoter locations. At some stage or other, certainly well before the 20th century when its effects began to be recognised, aerial pollution from the United States and Canada (and very likely, parts of Britain, depending on weather patterns at various times) must have been influencing the soils and vegetation of the Highlands. In this connection, it is most relevant that studies of the Galloway lochs 'showed acidification to have begun in the late 19th and early 20th centuries, fifty years before afforestation began', according to Neil Roberts' *The Holocene: An Environmental History* (Wiley-Blackwell, 1998). The effects of acid precipitation may not have been as obvious as in Sweden and Norway, for instance, but that does not mean that our countryside escaped.

Information on weather patterns would be interesting, too, in this context. As W.H. Pearsall pointed out (in *Mountains and Moorlands*), our soils would naturally become more acidic over time, but any periods of increased rainfall, or simply lower summer temperatures, would add to this effect. I am confident that within my lifetime the overall incidence of 'drying months' has certainly reduced, although the increasingly erratic patterns of recent years make firm conclusions difficult.

Increasing the acidity of an already acid soil can only make conditions less favourable to species already at, or approaching, the limit of their tolerance. Detailed distribution maps, comparing the presence of various species – whether of mosses and lichens, flowering plants, insect or bird species – over time, might well be interesting in this important context; someone must have some, somewhere?

I have referred to the numbers of grouse, now reduced from very high totals possibly to below their numbers prior to the formation of the sporting estates. Less easy to see perhaps, the numbers of the Atlantic salmon have certainly declined over the same period. When we were young, our parents knew the factor of the Assynt Estates well, and we often visited and sat in the sitting room with its big window overlooking Lochinver Bay. During many warm summers, with the rivers too low to tempt the fish, we watched the seething mass of salmon in the bay, many jumping, some skittering along on their tails, as they waited for the rain to swell the streams and let them up to spawn. I have not seen such a sight for decades.

Reasons for the decline in salmon numbers are quite well understood and include disease, parasites like the sea-louse, and netting at sea, but there can also be little doubt that chemical change in the river water may well affect the fertilising and hatching of eggs, and the feeding of tiny fish.

What has happened to the numbers of that other noble quarry species the red deer is, ironically, very different. I recall now, with considerable embarrassment, that I would gently explain to visitors from the United States why and how our system of deer control, our regulation of stalking, was so much better than the free-for-all that prevails across the Atlantic. I explained the strict, proprietorial attitudes of the landowners, and the role of our overseeing Government body, the Deer Commission. After a few decades, I was explaining why control of numbers by culling poorer specimens was tricky, in that it left the fitter animals to breed. And that significant culls resulted in better feeding for those who remained, leaving them healthier, and more successful in reproduction. Now, I just have to admit it – none of it has worked. There are far more deer than there have ever been and, more important than simple numbers, they are everywhere, including in places such as dense scrub, from which it is very difficult to remove them. And in the Highlands, scrub is, or should be, the mature native woodland of tomorrow.

Trying to assess the true effect of deer numbers (and sheep) on the overall state of our environment is not so easy. As far as the sheep are concerned, it is possible that the effect of their numbers has long been overestimated. That certainly has to be the conclusion drawn from careful study of West Coast woodlands, which probably should have disappeared decades ago when sheep numbers were at their height. But, largely, they did not. In any case, the numbers of sheep through most of the Highlands and Islands have clearly been reducing throughout the last forty years and, in most areas, are now irrelevant. As I have made clear, when the sheep move out, the deer move in, and the effect of the grazing of significant numbers of deer over a long period is generally agreed. I remember, in this context, my first sight of the grass under mature plantations of Scots pine, on the Mar Lodge Estate; there was less vegetation growing than on my father's lawn, and the smooth, short sward made the birch woodlands of Glenleraig (which used to be a sheep-farm) look tropically luxuriant. However, it cannot really be as simple as this; if you look at any old photographs taken of the Highlands, for instance, around 1930, the vegetation is generally much sparser than it is now. I have access to two of these pictures: one of my cottage, when it was the home of the shepherd; and one of my parents' house, when it was the same. In both, there are far fewer trees and bushes, there is much more bare rock, and what vegetation there is – heather and grasses – is much shorter, presumably as a result of higher grazing and more burning. Now, we have more deer, far more deer, and yet the overall state of the vegetation would appear to be better; the grass is certainly longer.

The problem is not simply the numbers of deer now ranging around the Highlands, it is where they are that counts, and the effect that their grazing will have on the regeneration of ancient woodlands, for instance. We have already seen that high levels of grazing by deer have removed nearly all the heather in Glen Shiel; it would be interesting to know what their effect was on flowering plants, and on berry species – do these get eaten out, too? The worrying problem is that, if so, they will not simply reappear because deer numbers are reduced, but may be totally shaded out by the increased volume of coarse grasses. Land management in the Highlands, if you are desperately concerned with the natural heritage, is (as the old joke goes) rather like taking directions from an Irishman: you would never start from here.

The relevant chapter of *Nature Contested* discusses all this – and more – but is, I suspect, not enough read, certainly not by those who perhaps have most need of reading it. It ends, as we so often do (and I already have), with the inevitable note that further research is needed. That is for sure, and I have some suggestions as to what we might look at and where. It seems to me that one of the constant conundrums through all this complicated debate is that some upland areas have markedly changed in the last 200 years, while we know that others have not, and although we may list and discuss some of the clearly relevant factors (as I have tried to do), most of us are not quite convinced that we have it sussed. I certainly am not.

We started this book with Assynt and John Home, and I will end this chapter again with that wonderful parish, and Home's most useful survey. In my account of a walk in Glenleraig, I referred to one particular sheiling, the Ruigh Dorcha. Home listed and mapped it and, as I say, it is still obviously fertile, green with grass and (sadly) bracken – and rather enjoyed by the deer. Home referred to some other places in this general area, some on the neighbouring farm of Nedd: 'The fine Brae of Wood next Glenlirag affords very rich Grass, as does also that beautiful Green Hill called Knock Goram lying at the East end of the Farm. All the other Hill Grounds are more barren but afford pretty good, dry, heathy Pasture.'

As may already be clear, I have known this area intimately since I was nine years old, and have walked over it for much of my life. The contrasts here are very interesting and, if we could only understand them, we might find at least part of the key to the question that has been the concern of this chapter. I can see no distinction of management or climate between the locations mentioned. The Ruigh Dorcha remains basically as Home saw it: green, fertile and dry. 'Knock Goram' (now, curiously, 'Gorm Cnoc' on the maps and locally) is one of a number of eminences: relatively small, craggy hills that stand above the general level of the 'plateau' of Lewisian Gneiss that lies between the great hills like Quinag and the sea. As Home suggests, there are others, such as Ghlas Cnoc, but I would never describe much of this Nedd hill–ground as 'dry'. And that 'beautiful Green Hill' is definitely no longer green. I have walked all around it many times, observed it from further off countless times, climbed over its summit from several directions, and from none has it ever, through all these years, looked green. Most of it is damp underfoot much of the time, and nearly all covered with the usual coarse grasses, sphagnum moss and odd bits of thin heather. Only on its lower slopes, above the lovely Gorm Loch Mor, and north-facing, is there anything different to see: some better heather, a few small rowan trees, a very little grass. Why has the green Ruigh Dorcha stayed green and dry, while under the same management and climatic conditions, the beautiful green hill of Gorm Cnoc has turned brown and largely uninviting? Is something different happening below ground? Is the Lewisian gneiss, which underlies both, differentiated by one or more volcanic dykes? Does the chemistry of the underground water vary? Are there glacial deposits under the grass of the sheiling? We need to be able to answer these types of question.

Fifteen

PROBLEMS OF
HIGHLAND LAND USE

The campaign by Victorian gamekeepers against all predators, highlighted in the previous chapter, is one of the defining attributes of the sporting estate of that era, wide in its ramifications, and still raises issues and questions today. The effect on the populations of predators is generally well known: a good number were made extinct, while some became very rare. Both the osprey and the red kite, for instance, were driven out. The osprey eventually staged its own comeback, with a little help from its human friends (by then rather more numerous than in the Victorian period), while the red kite has been reintroduced to a number of locations, beginning in the Black Isle, north of Inverness. Readers may have noticed that on my walks, I have generally managed to see some eagles. The sea eagle was another that became extinct and has been reintroduced, while golden eagles are somewhat unexpectedly frequent among the higher hills. Considering the low apparent productivity of the habitat, golden eagles in the West are in fact remarkably common; there are high densities in Mull and Skye, for instance. These populations are in reality artificially high, maintained to a significant extent by feeding extensively on carrion – the dead sheep to which I have occasionally referred (Mull and Skye still have quite high numbers of sheep) and dead deer, although live rabbits are also important.

We have almost two separate populations of golden eagle. Those on the West Coast, quite numerous, tend to have low success in breeding, presumably because of the amount of carrion they consume. In the Eastern Highlands, there is more live prey available, and the success rate is higher. The overall population density is, however, lower and this is largely the result of persecution, due to the fact that the 'live prey' may include game, like mountain hares and grouse.

Despite legal protection, the persecution of predators, especially birds of prey, continues. The red kites from the Black Isle, although breeding successfully, have failed to expand outside that area, which is largely surrounded by sporting estates. Every now and again there are successful prosecutions, and now that a proprietor is legally responsible for any such events on their land, one might hope that this sort of crime would decline. Further discussion of this is difficult at this time, as investigations are continuing into the deaths in Ross-shire in 2014 of twelve red kites and four buzzards (and several other birds of prey, more than twenty in all) which, one reads, 'may have been killed accidentally by pest control measures'.

Two things, however, may clearly be said on this issue. There is still, undoubtedly, persecution of protected birds of prey, and it remains a disgrace, a totally unacceptable persistence of the Victorian attitude, a most unhappy legacy. On the other hand, I find myself recalling that when I lived in Orkney in the early 1980s, I wrote and circulated a paper on a number of rural issues, including the poor relationship at that time between farmers and conservationists in the Islands. Reading recently (January 2015) that a Ross-shire proprietor, who claims that the vast majority of 'shepherds, farmers, crofters, ghillies, foresters, stalkers, gamekeepers and landowners in the Highlands' support wildlife conservation, has posted signs saying 'RSPB not welcome here', I am forced to conclude, with reluctance, that the entrenched positions of two all-too separate groups of people, remain rather firmly in place. That, too, is part of the legacy.

While the immediate result of the wholesale slaughter of predators was clearly an increase in the numbers of game, it would be quite logical to imagine that it must also have been followed by plagues of small mammals and enormously increased flocks of small birds. This would be likely enough, but I have never seen evidence for such changes. It is, presumably, possible that there were increases in the short term, but that the limitations of the food supply caused subsequent reductions. (Another area for further research?)

Despite the fairly obvious effects of the reduction of predators on grouse populations, for instance, food supply would remain critical. This can only ever be partly dependent on management actions, like muirburn, and is always heavily influenced by weather and how it changes from year to year. The fact that many populations of grouse appear in recent years to have tumbled from absurd totals to something approaching the levels when figures began to be kept (1834 in the Drumlanrig records) obscures, I think, the fact that the current levels are actually still artificially high, and surprisingly good news for the proprietors. We have, after all, seen that the moorland environment in the mid-1800s was dramatically more productive than it is currently. To maintain the present population, under far poorer conditions, at the level prevailing under those very favourable conditions is a considerable achievement, and one that is unlikely to continue given problems to which we have referred, like aerial pollution. It is almost inevitable that grouse numbers will further decline; it is to be hoped that birds of prey will not again be held responsible, especially as they will be subject to the same fundamental problems.

Persecution extended well beyond anything that we might possibly consider 'birds of prey'. It included, for instance, the dipper, on the suspicion that any bird feeding under water might be consuming fish eggs or tiny hatchlings. The dipper, too, has recovered (but to what extent, compared to its original populations, we may never know) and even though, as we have seen, salmon numbers have greatly declined, I have at least not heard of any demand that dippers should be controlled. Seals, common or grey, are a different matter, although the prevalence of salmon-farms is also relevant to the occasional demands for a reduction in their numbers. These are all rather over-simplistic solutions to decreasing populations, for which there may be many causes.

In recent decades, a link between forestry policy, the management of riverbanks and salmon populations seems to have been agreed, although, when walking or driving by many rivers, you might find little reason to believe it. While it is still debated whether salmon actually feed as they make their way upriver to spawn, there is no doubt at all that the next generation, in infancy, in the same rivers, actually does feed, and all sorts of fairly obvious insects, and other, rather less obvious invertebrates are crucial in this. These populations, in their turn, are very dependent on the riverside vegetation, particularly the trees, and so the habit of manicuring the riverbanks and cutting back bushes and trees, in order to facilitate access and casting, must clearly be harmful. For many decades, the growth of willow and alder alongside Highland rivers has been actively cut, or allowed to die through being eaten by stock or deer, but the cutting of riverside grass is a more recent absurdity, which may easily be seen on the Tay and Spey amongst other prestigious rivers.

It seems ridiculously difficult to persuade some fishers, and/ or fishery managers, to regard river systems as anything other than simply a conduit for one creature, the migratory salmon, which they want to catch. Even though the numbers they may catch must clearly depend on the number of fry, parr and smolts that survive to go to sea and they obviously rely on the overall health of the river environment, the obvious connection does not often seem to be made or, if it is, not much gets done about it. Admittedly, some measures, like re-establishing riparian woodland where it has disappeared (yet more fences against sheep and deer!), can be difficult and expensive, but there is no real alternative. Too often, short-term fixes are used instead: burn a little more heather on a grouse moor, shoot a few cormorants on the river.

At their best, these river environments can be rich, beautiful and entrancing. In 2000, I was part of a small expedition in North American canoes down the River Spey, along with a group of fellow environmentalist writers, singers, poets and thinkers. I made a few notes while paddling along the upper reaches, from which I quote: 'That journey did provide some moments of magic, and produced, at the very least, an awareness of the natural abundance of such long, riparian habitats; I had no idea there could be so many common sandpipers in the world! I remember a day with light on the river, the long curves of its green shore bisected all the time by the low flickering flights of the little waders, the plaintive, constant piping which I heard again at night in my dreams.' Today, I find myself wondering whether the sandpipers were shot like the dippers – just in case.

While waterside bushes and trees were being removed, native woodlands of birch, rowan and hazel were often being replaced by plantations of the 'new' trees, which had been found to grow well, although Scots pine and larch were often included. Towards the wetter West, it was perhaps simply the Sitka that was used and, through succeeding years, especially after the wholesale felling during World War I, great acreages of these trees were imposed on the Highland landscape – another complete transformation of the natural environment. As has been explained, selective thinning was virtually abandoned as a result of Government parsimony and countless plantations, large and small, dank and inhospitable, remain in our countryside. They were often planted right down to the waterside; this at least is no longer permitted, as it has been deduced that it increases run-off after rain and also may increase acidity when compared to the more absorbent effects of deciduous leaf-litter. Many remain, however, and to remove them will involve clear-felling, and the likelihood of soil erosion, with more silt running into and clogging up the gravelly spawning beds. Remedying past, fundamental errors in the countryside is not a simple task.

It was eventually recognised that there had been a considerable over-emphasis on the planting of conifers, and a real neglect of native species and the 'semi-natural' woods they make up. ('Semi-natural' is almost as endearing a term as 'SSSI', the Site of Special Scientific Interest, is it not? – how often we shoot ourselves in the foot, when we need to be engaging public interest!) Earnest bodies and enthusiastic campaigning put that right, and for some decades there has been an official enthusiasm for these long-neglected habitats. Sadly, owing to the success of the Victorian's third principal quarry species, the 'iconic' red deer, most of that progress has been within high fences, and the 'natural' or 'wild' nature of the Scottish Highlands put beyond redemption. And if that were not enough, a close examination of these flagships for conservation, these native woods, old and new, makes for sad reading.

For a start, the Forestry Commission's Native Woodland Survey of Scotland has shown that deer have got into our native woodlands, fenced or unfenced, in such numbers as to threaten their future. 'A third show high or very high damage by grazing, and that is largely down to deer,' says Andrew Fairbairn of Woodland Trust Scotland. As I have shown, grazing outside the current boundaries of any old wood is potentially as harmful to its future as grazing within it. It is admitted we have a problem: on the one hand, people like deer and deer are woodland animals but, to our overall Highland environment, the loss of our ancient woodlands would be as tragic as the Highland Clearances were, in social terms. Solving a problem like this will not be made any easier by the predictable chorus from certain quarters that deer are being rendered extinct, and there will be no jobs in future for stalkers and gamekeepers. Given the fact that we now have somewhere in the region of half a million red deer, that the population will always need to be carefully counted and culled, and that the most effective predator of deer has two legs and carries a gun, those claims are simple nonsense.

But the bad news does not stop there. For far too long, the emphasis, as far as our woods are concerned, has been on quantity rather than quality. The problem is seen at every level. Many of our flagship old woodland places, like Abernethy, contain large areas that are endless, even-aged, monocultural, mossy and dull – a huge contrast to the wood I described on our Speyside walk. New planted woods in Assynt and Coigach are species-poor; there will be some birch (often better regenerating than planted), rowan, a few hazel and holly perhaps (often just where they will be seen), and quite a lot of Scots pine, despite the fact that it has not grown in these parishes for perhaps as much as 4,000 years. A prolonged, fairly recent spell of wet, mild, windy winters virtually turned them into deciduous trees. Alder is planted in places where it could never have seeded itself; it makes a show for some years, and then will die without being able to regenerate. The only justification for planting it – other than the psychological one, that it actually visibly grows in the first few years – must be that by fixing nitrogen from the air it enriches the soil. I have long suggested that after a few years, successful clumps of alder should be interplanted with willow, as an experiment to see whether this really achieves anything useful. The critical point about nearly all these new woods is that they are far poorer in species than the woods surviving around them and that, often enough, it is price that determines what is planted. There is too much commitment to planting new areas, however unsuitable some of them may look – as in Rum, it would be better to assist in the conversion of plantation into something more closely resembling woodland.

The question of woodland composition is important; I have never understood why the species that happen to be less common now, after thousands of years of complicated history – like (on the West Coast) bird cherry, wych elm, guelder rose – should not, in appropriate places, be planted in considerable numbers. We need woods of great diversity, reflecting all the local species, not just the ones, like birch, that happen to be most common now (in any case, they should be left to cater for themselves – i.e. regenerate as and when they like). Where it is appropriate to plant pine, as the conservation charity Trees for Life is doing over wide areas, it is important that they should be planted with a real number of other species. As pine grows, it tends to shade out the surrounding deciduous trees until a pine monoculture is reached, as may be seen all over the Highlands. It was fire, the ripping through of fire, maybe only once every three or four hundred years, that burnt the flammable pine, cre-ated the open gaps in the canopy, let light on to the woodland floor, burnt the deposit of needles to create a good seed bed, which let the deciduous opportunists, like rowan and birch, back into the game. The heat from the fires opened the pine cones, released the seed, the baby pines started to grow slowly, and the whole, natural process started up again… If we cannot replicate natural woods, and natural processes like episodes of fire, we can at least, and should, plant woods that are as varied as possible. In any case, planting pine in the acid areas that it tolerates (which is much of the Highlands, if not too wet) in 'soils' that have been made more acid by aerial pollution (which has not ceased) and which the pine will make yet more acid, even if only through the deposition of its needles, will do absolutely nothing to recreate the woodland 'fertility' of which some folk dream. Trees, although I love them, and have studied them in some depth, are not a panacea in themselves, and the wrong tree, planted in the wrong place, is simply a wasted effort. It still happens; I have seen silver birch planted in bog on the West Coast – and the public paid for it.

In connection with the composition of our woods, Richard Mabey (for instance in *BBC Wildlife*, March 2014) has recently and cogently been urging that in face of all the threats to our native species, from exotic pests whether insect or fungal, we completely reconsider our planting policies, and aim for high and local diversity. I agree; treating the British Isles or the Scottish Highlands as some sort of Noah's Ark carrying only the purest of native species, struggling to eliminate all infiltrators, is no longer feasible and probably distracts us from the bigger, critical issues which face us all in the early 21st century.

I have repeatedly referred to the real problem of deer, and the urgent need to control their numbers. Many of us might be able to agree on at least one simple step: the 'artificial' feeding of deer during the winter, whether with hay or cattle cobs or whatever, should be made illegal. But that would only achieve a return to something like natural mortality rates. In order to prepare a sensible response to other, more dramatic suggestions, we must return to those fundamental conclusions, reached in the last chapter: that the general environment of the Scottish Highlands and Islands was infinitely richer in the mid-1800s than it is now. Yes, there are now lots more deer but, otherwise, the environment is much poorer, and it makes no sense at all to introduce any more predators into it. I am not trying to object in retrospect to the reintroduction of the birds of prey like the red kite and the sea eagle, but I am absolutely clear that no more such reintroductions can be justified. I am, however, fundamentally opposed to the reintroduction of the wolf and, probably, to a lesser extent, the lynx.

Our problem is quite clearly a lack of the small birds and mammals that sustained the high predator levels of the 1830s, and culling deer will not magically restore thousands of birds to our moors. In any case, it must be clear that it would take seriously high numbers of wolves to have any impact whatsoever on half a million red deer, to say nothing of the sika, fallow and roe. When much more spacious countries such as Norway, Sweden or France struggle to retain large carnivores, in a small country like Scotland, where, as we have seen, wildlife crime is a constant reality, such ideas make no sense. Ecologically, the wolf would probably spell the end of the already-threatened ground-nesting birds, like the black grouse and capercaillie, as well as the red- and black-throated divers of which we are so proud. They already struggle to cope with the greater numbers we now see of badgers, otters and pine marten, free at last from the intense persecution of the Victorian gamekeepers. Wolves might well reduce the numbers of deer, but no one will persuade me that they would not also take a lone sheep or lambs, and eggs or chicks in a nest would make a nice appetiser if encountered. Carnivores are successful because they are omnivores and opportunists; we certainly do not need any more.

In conclusion, lest there be any doubt, the Highlands of the present day bear almost no resemblance to the Highlands the wolves frequented, and in which they became extinct in the late 1600s and early 1700s. To reintroduce them would, ecologically and socially, be totally irresponsible. It is a romantic dream.

Sixteen

A DRIVE UP STRATH GLASS
AND STRATH FARRAR

Today, we are not going for a walk; instead we are going for a drive through the lovely country that lies on the north side of Loch Ness, but southwest from Inverness. We start in Beauly, a bustling small town, or large village depending on where you were brought up. It is another of the estate villages and, even to this day, a glance in the telephone book reveals that an astonishing number of Frasers live in and around it. It is much older than that would suggest as, completely unseen to most visitors, it lies on the smooth-flowing river of the same name, and once had a small harbour; we are close to where the river enters the Firth. Near the site of the harbour are the sandstone remains of an old priory, possessed of a long nave and some interesting windows. It belonged to a rather obscure order of monks, the Valliscaulians, and was part of the 'civilising' of the wild Highlands in the 12th and 13th centuries, when the Canmore dynasty of Scottish kings began to move away from their Celtic origins.

Be that as it may, what you see here, apart from the ruins of the priory itself, is an attractive square of neat sandstone houses. Let us imagine that we spent the night in the Lovat Arms Hotel, externally a most interesting building, rather French in style, with fine windows and elaborate dormers in the steep, slated roof. We might cross the busy road to look in at Campbells, to say a quick hello and admire the beautiful bales of cloth, tartan and tweed on their dark shelves. Generations of many families, like my own grandparents and parents, received the most courteous of welcomes from the equivalent generations of the Campbell family, who ran it until very recently.

Once in the car, we soon leave the sandstone villas, passing through extensive new building before crossing the railway and heading briefly along the heavy, fertile, level ground. Very soon there is a junction, and if we turned to the left, a fine Telford bridge built in 1814 would take us across the river. The road and its bridges, along with the later railway, were all part of the enormous improvement in Highland infrastructure that facilitated the Victorian opening-up of the North, and allowed access to the developing estates. All this is part of the land of the Frasers of Lovat, whose principal seat was for a long time at nearby Beaufort Castle, a French name (like Beauly), which reflects the influence of the Normans who were brought in during the 12th century, another period of development and significant social change in the Highlands. Beaufort is on an old site; the present building, which may occasionally be glimpsed through the trees of its surrounding parkland, reflects a building campaign of the 1880s.

At the junction we turn right and uphill, soon passing yet more development: the works associated with the recent upgrading of the Beauly-Denny electrical transmission lines – tall pylons walking off into the wooded distance. Below the road on the left is a hydro dam, part of an earlier phase. The Falls of Kilmorack were a famed beauty spot, where my grandmother and grandfather got engaged; the falls disappeared when the river was dammed here, one of a series that controls the flow almost all the way from the watershed far to the west. The dams were provided with facilities, ladders and lifts to enable migrating salmon to move up to their spawning grounds; only later, I think, were grilles placed to prevent young fish, on their way back down the river, from passing through the blades of the turbines and being killed.

All this area is well wooded, with some native trees like hazel, alder and birch between the road and the river, often massed conifers above. In the winter, there are good views of the long dark pools, perhaps of goldeneye, or the occasional goosander. The latter, like its close relative the merganser, was much persecuted by gamekeepers, as they do undoubtedly catch small fish in their narrow, serrated bills. It is to be hoped that such birds are monitored by the RSPB as closely as are the more glamorous birds of prey.

Soon, we pass another dam and enter into an area of really tall trees; below us, the river flows deep and slow, through a gorge. It is worth stopping for a look. I once did so and was rewarded with one of those quick, spectacular, wild moments that stay with you forever. It so happened that an osprey had decided to fly along the dark river below the cliffs, when it was suddenly attacked by a peregrine falcon. Wildly flapping its great wings, the osprey called continuously in alarm, while the peregrine, screaming in anger, repeatedly assailed it. The two birds, noisily entangled, spiralled up and over my head, eventually disappearing over the horizon (but still audible for several more minutes).

On the right, briefly, we see the neat cottages – some with elaborate woodwork – of the Crask of Aigas, the village of another smaller estate. There was a waterfall here, too, before the construction of the dam. An island, almost impossible to see from this side, occupies an extraordinarily picturesque if restricted position at the entrance to the gorge. Eilean Aigas played its own role in establishing the haze of romance with which the Victorians shrouded the reality of the Highland clans: it was for a time the home of two English brothers who claimed illegitimate descent from Bonnie Prince Charlie using, latterly, the surname of Stuart. They patently hoped to cash in on the enthusiasm for all things Scottish and Highland and for a while did, although they failed, apparently, to persuade Sir Walter Scott of their authenticity. The Lord Lovat of the day, however, must have been convinced as he permitted them to live in a 'hunting-lodge' on the island, where they held some sort of gloomy Celtic court. In particular, they published a number of books, one of which, *Vestiarium Scoticum* (1842), illustrated several tartans that were, up to that point, completely unknown, and have since been almost unanimously agreed to have derived from the colourful imagination of the brothers.

The history of the island has not exactly been dull since. Compton Mackenzie, the author whose works include some wonderful fantasies based on a fictitious clan chief, Donald MacDonald of Ben Nevis (the inspiration for the television series *Monarch of the Glen*, filmed around Ardverikie), lived there for a few years from 1930. His wife, Faith, particularly loved the wonderful setting and luxuriant, scented garden.

In recent years, the estate was purchased first by a Malaysian businessman, and then by a Canadian, who altered the fairly modest old house and also constructed a new mansion in an imposing and elaborate style. One can only presume that the romance lingers to some effect... In 2012, it was widely reported to be for sale for £15 million, but subsequently was reported to have sold for a fifth of that price.

Immediately after the village of the Crask, the road swings around a corner high above the river and the scene opens out (this is what the Anglicised word 'crask' means). The view is wonderful and features, prominently, the warm sandstone of that elegant, authentic Victorian lodge, the House of Aigas, set on a wide sunny level, surrounded by fine trees, above fields that descend to the wide waters of the river.

From here, we drive gently along for a while, with occasional good views of the river pools; it meanders wonderfully for much of this section, through what is effectively a long 'nature reserve' of old ox-bow 'lakes', gentle back-waters and long-abandoned channels, all edged with alder and willow. Fortunately, it has escaped total 'improvement', even keeping most of its waterside trees, although there has at times been pressure to make things easier for the fishers along its length. The hillsides have changed quite a lot, though. My one-inch map of 1969 shows a few discrete woods along the roadsides, plantations that might well derive from the Victorian times; these are now pretty well continuous. (Other things change, too: that map cost only 44p!)

The road narrows and we enter some trees; on the left there is a planted oak wood, part of the policies of the next big house. The 'new house' of Aigas was built by industrialists, a family from Glasgow. But Erchless, which we are approaching (*Rhododendron ponticum* beginning to appear along the verges), is an old castle, home of the Chisholms for generations until 1935. In the Victorian period, its tall tower acquired another substantial wing, and the estate was embellished with a fine farm square, one or two rows of cottages and a splendid avenue. The castle is hard to see from the road in the winter, impossible in the summer when there are leaves on the big trees; the old public road ran along the front, but was later moved so as to ensure its privacy. It is my understanding that the clan still owns a small area beside the public road; this is also worth a visit. Initially, as the visitor gently ascends what appears to be a precisely curved small valley (resembling a hollow-way in the south of England), it is not at all clear where you are – the tops of the banks are masked by trees and more rhododendron, although this gets cut at intervals. Then, on the left, some steps take you up to a flat, circular space, with a few big trees and several impressive gravestones, marking the resting place of members of the family of the clan chiefs. It is not immediately obvious but this is the site of a fortification that long preceded the tower of Erchless down the hill; this is a motte, of the 12th century, another relic of the Norman presence in this area. It is called Cnoc an Taighe Mhoir, or 'the (flat-topped) hill of the big house'. Presumably the motte was crowned by a substantial hall, set within a wall or surrounding palisade.

Some of the stones are high, Celtic-style crosses, embellished with a deeply carved, interlacing pattern. The grass is always neatly cut, the mosses luxuriant, the place mostly shaded by the high trees. The atmosphere is, perhaps appropriately, slightly melancholy in a romantic Victorian way.

Continuing along the now rather narrower road, we reach another junction. Were we to cross the tributary river here and drive directly on, we would soon reach that section of Strath Glass which, fault-guided (parallel to Loch Ness and the Great Glen Fault) and straight-sided, gives it its name: the trench or furrow-like glen. I used to live in this section and if, on a soft summer evening, I climbed the extremely steep slopes above my house to reach the gentler hill above, only then did I become conscious that Strath Glass runs through a plateau of high moorland, cutting through that elevated land exactly like the trench its name implies. The black grouse used to lek up there, bowing, strutting, parading and fighting, making all the time an extraordinarily compelling, carrying, churring sound.

We are, however, taking the road to the right, before the bridge; it indicates 'Glen Strathfarrar' but as a strath is merely a wide glen, I am reluctant to endorse the implicit tautology. In any case, the element of this name that really matters is the 'Farrar'. As a linguist, I enjoy exploring place-names, and have, occasionally, hit on moderately convincing derivations, but the doyen of Scottish place-name studies is W.F.H. Nicolaisen, before whose depth of scholarship I stand abashed. He spends a few pages of *Scottish Place-names* (Batsford, 1976) on the name 'Farrar', which, as 'Varar', appears on a map by the cartographer Ptolemy in 150 AD, making it convincingly pre-Norse, pre-Gaelic, pre-Pictish. A name, therefore, of the greatest antiquity; in 150 AD, it applied to the whole system, including what might be called the 'ultimate' estuary, the Moray Firth.

Having now turned to follow the river of that name, we stop at a gate; the road onwards is private, maintained by the local hydroelectric company, which has power stations up the strath, and the relevant estates. The gate-keeper is apparently not paid to manage the gate from the 1st of November through to late March, during which period access appears to have to be negotiated but seems still to be reasonably simple.

Once, then, let through the locked gate, we proceed gently up the narrow road, which has a few potholes in sections. At first, there is a deer farm on the right, and then a pleasing lodge set back against a hill covered mostly in birch. Such a wood, single-species and glorious in autumn colours, is likely to be secondary, the result of rapid colonisation by the silver birch, following a major felling. The original wood probably included many oaks, being in quite a fertile and sunny location. Some remain. Further up, we have glimpses of the river, and start to become aware of beautiful, round-topped old pines appearing on the southern bank. Then there is a flat, grassy zone, usually complete with sheep. Some sort of trench runs through the area and, if you follow it, there is a larger, hollow place, said to be the site of a bobbin-mill, where some of the wood was cut to provide necessities for the spinning and weaving industries. The woods in Strath Farrar are among the many (including Rothiemurchus, Loch Maree and Loch Lomond) that were extensively exploited, but retain some beautiful, mixed woodland. As we carry on up the road, it is mostly birch on our more accessible side of the river, with the splendour of the pines on the darker, southern bank.

In the autumn, this section of the strath can be glorious, the birch all golden, the considerable bracken growth light red to russet, some aspen brilliant yellow against the darkest green of the massed pine. We often stop to have a short walk along the river to listen out for flocks of tits, which might just contain some of the lively cresties, to look for the tell-tale, bobbing white patch of a dipper (why do so many waterside birds bob?), or perhaps to see a salmon. Once or twice, out of the mysterious, peaty black waters, flecked with foam in back-water drifts, there has appeared the silent, sinister, shining red back of a big, late fish.

Soon, there are pines on our side of the river and much juniper under them on the other, then some oak. There are a few exclosures as well, and places full of vigorous regeneration, which were previously fenced. This is another place where reconciling the presence of substantial numbers of deer with the cycle of renewal of the woodland has proved difficult in the past, and impossible without fencing. Like Inverpolly, Strath Farrar was once a National Nature Reserve, and has lost that symbolic status. It is not as diverse a habitat as that lovely wood we walked to above Loch Morlich, but it does have a significant mix of species, including some truly fine oaks.

After another dam, we enter into a more open zone, with the pine continuing along the steep southern shore, and larger bodies of water. Soon, we enter the ground of another estate, that of Braulen. It was formerly part of the extensive Lovat holdings but, according to an article of November 2014 by Helen Webster on www.walkhighlands.co.uk, it now belongs to 'Andras Ltd, which is reputedly owned by a wealthy Malaysian. The company also owns the 42,000-acre Glenavon

Estate near Tomintoul in the Cairngorms. Both are run as sporting estates.' The owners have chosen to plant, at intervals along the road up to Braulen Lodge, pairs (one each side) of specimen trees, some of which at least are certainly oak. They have to be protected from the deer, of course, and some were planted in inappropriate ground (like oak in a bog) and have not come to much. Being single trees, they may suffer from the wind whistling down from the big hills; it is hard to know exactly what the result of this planting will look like. Although it does seem a somewhat inappropriate notion for this Highland glen – something out of southern parkland, for instance – it has to be admitted that previous owners have also done strange things, which most people do not even notice. Further along the road, after a loch with a densely planted island, there is an empty house and, close by it, a small group of tall lime trees (*Tilia*), which is equally odd.

A little beyond this, and ignored by nearly all visitors, on the steep slope above the road and the riverbank below it, are several splendid old alder trees. Many of them have short, thick trunks, columnar in style, and wide-spreading branches, without much height. They are growing there because, I think, a volcanic dyke, rich in minerals, crosses the strath here. It is certainly free-draining, providing good conditions for the retention of trees. The shape of these is very distinct; I interpret them as old pollards – alder was valued for its strength and lightness, and the fact that if placed in wet ground, as in a fence or gate, for instance, it would not rot. In fact, it often grew!

Shortly after this, we swing around a bend, with glorious views of the big hills in front of us if the weather is kind. In the foreground are the 'Braulen flats': a wide, open, level area, which once must have been a lake-bed, through which the river now meanders, in essence very similar to the burn in Glenleraig beside the 'dark sheiling' (in both locations, older, higher drainage channels can be identified). Some of the ground here is damp, but some other parts are dry enough to support genuine green grass, which is now cut, encouraging new growth every spring, on which the large numbers of deer feed. The same is true of a few locations further down the strath. This is the sort of deer-feeding of which I can only approve; it attracts them into an area that should be able to cope with both grazing and the trampling while, at the same time, lifting the pressure on the many important remnants of the pine wood – most of them across the strath.

We reach Braulen itself, a fairly modest lodge, built of the pleasing sandstone from down around Beauly. In this area, whooper swans have often over-wintered and one, apparently injured, never left. It managed to find a mate, an ordinary mute swan, and they subsequently raised offspring, an interesting hybrid. I find myself wondering why this large, apparently quite fertile area, possessed of attractive damp places that must surely swarm with invertebrates, never seems to attract any waders, like curlew, lapwing or dunlin – or even greenshank, that most elegant of birds, whose clear piping overhead used to fill me with the joys of spring.

One autumn, however, Strath Farrar was an astonishing place. It was an average sort of day, not one of the golden glory-days of autumn, but dry and pleasant enough, despite a hint of coldness to come. The aspen and birch had lost their beauty rather early but, in one of those strange inversions of normal timing, a few rowans were still heavy with berries of deepest scarlet. The rowans were, however, far from plentiful enough to be the attraction for the number of birds we saw, just emerging from the grass and the heather as we made our very slow way downstream from Braulen. There were some fieldfares – big, loud, colourful, bossy thrushes – but they were totally outnumbered by their smaller relations, the redwings.

These are neat birds, just smaller and darker than a song thrush when seen from above, handsome though, with a clear, light eye-stripe on the dark head. It is when they fly that the red underwing is most conspicuous. It makes for a most attractive bird, often seen in the Scottish winter. On this occasion, there were untold thousands of them, constantly rising from the ground, all around, ahead of us and behind us. Wherever you looked, there were more; whenever you thought we must have seen the last of them, another huge flock lifted off the ground, on this side and that. It continued like this right down the strath till we entered the woods, when numbers began to thin out.

It was an astonishing occasion, the appearance of a relatively common bird in numbers that none of us had ever experienced. Thinking about it later, I realised that it gave us a glimpse of the natural world as it was seen before and during the Victorian era, when, as Chris Smout describes in *Nature Contested*, 'about 22,000 wheatears were taken annually around Eastbourne', 'great numbers' of ring ousels were seen in Upper Deeside in June, and 'flocks of hundreds' of dotterel were recorded on spring migration. One thing cannot be doubted: in the last 200 or so years, our single species, in a whole number of ways, has hugely impoverished the natural world we inherited. To continue (as we are) on that same course, right across this planet, is not simply folly – it is sacrilege.

Seventeen

THE MOVEMENT
FROM THE LAND

We have seen that places quite close to the coast, like Glenleraig, and far inland, like Glencalvie, were 'cleared' throughout the period when the sporting estates were being established. I would love to see a map of the whole of the Highlands and Islands with every such area clearly marked. It would be a huge work of research, but the impact of such a map would be significant. On a local level, in Assynt, we do have the Home Survey and maps, with every farm of that period clearly shown, and it is astonishing how well populated the now–empty hinterland was. However illogical it may really be, there is still some degree of emotional reaction when you come across such a place, miles from anywhere, reached by no convenient track, but with patches of fertile ground still showing, and old walls standing a few stones in height. These places were once home to a family or families, the scenes of daily activity – hard and unending though it may have been.

The Clearances were, of course, the major episode of local depopulation throughout the Highlands and Islands, but not the last. It is well known that a huge number of the remaining menfolk from the whole area went to fight in the Great War; memorials in every village and parish testify to the carnage, which was another wave of depopulation. When I was young, throughout Assynt there were many spinsters, then ageing, which clearly reflected the simple lack of men to marry. Around the same time, there was a distinct contraction of the remaining population, a withdrawal from the remotest corners, the places where it was hardest to live and men were needed to sustain everyday life. All over the Highlands and Islands during this time, families started leaving small islands, or the wilder stalkers' or shepherds' cottages. Their ruins can still be seen in many places; the corrugated-iron roof will have rusted or blown off, but the strong gable walls still stand. Often that is all there is, apart from the pathos of a place-name that once meant something – everything – to someone.

Rather less noticed, there was another wave of depopulation after World War II. Although fewer went to fight, many still did, and, unlike those who served and normally died in the trenches, these folk, both men and women this time, went all over the globe during the course of hostilities. Most of them saw something of the world, and more of them returned, changed by where they had been and what they had seen. It may have been the result of their changed ideas about life, or sheer economic necessity, but a great number of them left, either to go back around the world, or to the big industrial cities further south. In my youth, it seemed that most local families had relations either in Canada or Glasgow, or both. You may still see abandoned crofts and houses from this period, especially in the middle of the country, which has since proved less attractive to those whose search for a second or retirement home (like my parents) has kept a house inhabited and masked another move away from the land.

In recent years, the population of the Highlands and Islands has actually been growing, but that increase hides changes. The centres like Fort William, Inverness, Kirkwall or Lerwick have been growing as, locally, have Gairloch and Dounby, but there is, again, a contraction, a move to cluster together where the services are, the schools and supermarkets. In the 1980s I lived very happily in Birsay, at the far northwest corner of Mainland Orkney. Compared to the distances being travelled then in the Highlands, the ten minutes' drive to Dounby, at the heart of the West Mainland, or the half-hour to Kirkwall, was nothing, and it never occurred to us that we were in any way 'out of it all', cut off or remote. But now, my friends and former neighbours report that several of the houses in the little village close by are empty, including, most of the time, the one where we lived and ran a small but lively business. There is, slowly and far less obviously perhaps, yet another wave of depopulation here. Even where homes are still maintained, if the occupants are actually working rather than retired, patterns of employment are changing and far fewer than before are actually working on the land.

In former days, when the remoter places were still occupied, life was certainly not easy. If you were a shepherd or keeper (or both together, it was a common combination), your wages would not be high, reflecting for a start the fact that the estate provided you with a house. A real measure of self-sufficiency was required as winter snow, which in years gone by might last for several weeks, could easily cut you off from all external supplies. For fuel, peat was often cut, dried and stacked. You might keep a house-cow for milk (although tinned milk was commonplace), and the cow, grazing around the place in the summer, would require hay in the winter, which an enclosed park and some hard work would supply. There would, at the very least, be a potato patch, perhaps a strip of turnips, sometimes for man and beast. Crofters at the time quite often grew oats, too. A keeper who was not officially a shepherd might still keep some sheep of his own, and would kill one or two to see the family through the winter. I remember an old couple who ordered a sack or two of oatmeal and a barrel of herrings, and that, basically, fed them through the long, cold months.

The restrictions of this life make it clear why many abandoned it when they could, but it had one significant, ecological benefit that would be reflected in the wildlife around. This was all about small-scale agriculture; there was something of a mess, a manure heap perhaps, a bale or two of old hay. Even if on a small scale, ground was turned over: I have little doubt that weeds and wildflowers flourished along with the potatoes and turnips, and grass was cut to grow anew. The hay-meadows, small as they may have been, never saw weedkillers, and were full of flowers; I remember the butterflies dancing above the massed blooms of red and white clover, bees buzzing in the tangled vetches. Crofting communities in this period had partridge and corn bunting in the modest strip of arable, snipe at the bottom of the wetter fields. Harriers came around looking for mice and rats. Red grouse and black game came out of the heather or birch woods to clean up any fallen grain. It was no paradise, except on occasional, wonderful days, but there was life in the house, and life around it. Now, I see places where two stone gables stand, rough moorland grass up to the walls, and all is quiet.

The point is that these now-abandoned cottages required small-scale agriculture to survive, and that is good for wildlife. The most critical activity, as far as long-term agriculture is concerned in the Highlands, is turning the soil over. On our drive up Strath Glass and Strath Farrar we saw nothing, in agricultural terms, other than pasture – grass. Very often, all there is to be seen is fields of cropped grass, each with a handful of sheep, sometimes cattle. The problem is that in our wet climate with so few drying days, the trampling of hooves, heavy and light, year in, year out, causes compaction of the soil, which impedes its drainage and reduces the number of invertebrates. The only thing to benefit from this is the soft rush that slowly invades wet pastures, ultimately smothering the grass in a dense growth that gives almost no benefit to stock or to wildlife. Despite its rather beguiling name, it is remarkably hard to eliminate, and fertilising the fields merely feeds the rush.

The main pest of dry ground, on the other hand, is the bracken. Handsome when dying, it is otherwise an absolute nuisance, covering hillsides and drier fields, obliterating the flowers of the old hayfields and shading out nearly all seedling trees. It used to be cut for bedding for the cattle, and their weight, concentrated on relatively small hooves, flattened and cut its tender young shoots, using up a lot of the plant's energy. Now it covers an area much larger than does the dreaded *ponticum* and less effort is made to eradicate it, even though the places where it grows would make, for instance, a prime spot for a new oak wood. Like the rushes, bracken is difficult to remove once established; the alternatives are strong weedkillers, or a lot of very hard work cutting or bashing the young fronds. Sadly, many parts of the Highlands and Islands are too rough and rocky for easy cutting by machine. Some people have got into the habit of burning the old bracken during the next spring, but this merely fertilises it. Like rushes, bracken is of very little benefit to wildlife.

There are many glens and straths in the Highlands and Islands, and they reach far inland. In most of them, the tendency towards permanent pasture, and the prevalence of rushes and bracken, will be clear, but there are probably few people who have kept photographs of one location and can show the difference forty years has made, as I have. For much of our area, that fundamental change away from active, small-scale agriculture has been slow, and often unremarked. John Lister-Kaye, who has lived in Strath Glass for forty years, has often mentioned it; even if his message had really been taken on board, it is not completely clear what should be done. It is one thing to establish that this change within our glens must take its place with all the other changes mentioned in previous chapters and that it, too, has played a part in reducing, for instance, the number of waders breeding in wet meadows inland, but it is another to know how to mitigate it.

During recent decades, the effect of reduced gamekeeping, especially on the mammals judged to be vermin, has been marked. We now see, and enjoy seeing, significant numbers of badgers, otters and pine martens. They are attractive, lively and opportunistic omnivores, whose very presence would make it more difficult for birds like curlew to re-establish themselves in the glens, were other factors somehow to improve. After such extreme persecution as clearly took place in the heyday of the Victorian estate, most of us would be very reluctant to see an attempt to control numbers of any of those three, and, we might argue, with good reason. For a start, as should have been made entirely clear through the preceding chapters, we have not the faintest idea what a 'natural balance' of species in this landscape would be. It might be argued that we have tinkered enough with nature, and should be wary of further reductions of species that, only recently, were close to extinction. Throughout the history of human involvement with the natural world, there have been what are blithely referred to as 'unintended consequences'. The Victorian passion for deer has surely had exactly such unintended consequences, and our attempts to reduce significantly that inflated population will have others. A lack of dead deer and sheep in Skye and Mull is likely, as has been noticed, to reduce the local population of golden eagles, unless the rabbit population conveniently explodes. Longer heather, grasses and sedges may reduce the ability of the greenshank to find the invertebrates on which it feeds, and so the effort of improving the overall health of the landscape may reduce the numbers of some very special creatures. In every way, this is not easy territory.

For the Victorians, this landscape clearly had a romantic appeal, which helped to popularise the Highlands and encourage the creation of the Highland estate. It will have been noticed that new owners from around the world have bought into this dream, while the State, in the shape of the Department of Agriculture and the Forestry Commission, has long been a proprietor within the same area. Environmental charities too, like the RSPB, have a major role. The good which politicians achieve is often obliterated by the mistakes they make, and it is already often overlooked that Tony Blair's New Labour Government gave devolution to Scotland, and that an early Scottish Government gave the Highlands a measure of land and access reform, which has brought communities too into landholding and management. The fact of individual or corporate ownership, their own private aspirations, and the reality of distinct financial constraints and targets (awkward as they often are) mean that many of the most grandiose of aspirations for this land are sometimes doomed or, at the least, much reduced through time.

One such, very current, romantic passion is that for 'rewilding'. It seems to mean returning land, such as unused farmland, to a 'wild' or 'natural' state, sometimes then stocking it with creatures that have long been absent, such as herbivores like moose, or carnivores like the wolf. I think that I have said quite enough about the wolf, but also have to confess that I am not very excited about adding to the already enormous numbers of herbivores that we are struggling to control. In most cases, it is admitted that the introduction of creatures like the moose will not be considered for many years, if not decades.

I have visited one estate dedicated to the rewilding cause. Alladale (which seems to be a case of 'rewilding in a hurry') had put up an awful lot of fences and exposed a great deal of bare peat when I was there. Extremely beautiful though it is, Alladale did not then feel very wild to me. Nor did an article in *BBC Wildlife* (Summer 2013), by George Monbiot, convince me that he has much understanding of how our uplands actually work. If you remove sheep, then any nearby deer will move in and very little will change. If there are few or no deer, there will be no great regeneration, even if there is an adequate seed source (which often there is not). Ungrazed grassland just grows longer, and regeneration into it tends to be very poor or non-existent, and very limited in species. Rushes and bracken, on the other hand, as we have seen, do quite well. As I have said, this is not easy territory.

In the debate (where it exists) over 'what we should do with our countryside', there seem to have been, in recent years, two schools of thought. That at least is what I deduce when I read a comment by Richard Mabey, towards the end of *The Ash and the Beech* (Vintage, 2007). The context is a realisation that 'natural disturbances were an entirely normal and well-tolerated part of a woodland's experience', with which I can only agree (and I would even include the effects of fire although I realise that, given the discrete and limited extent of our individual woods, we are most unlikely to have the courage 'to let it rip'). He continues, 'It prompted changes in conservation policy, too... Its furthest ripples have even reached the Wildlife Trusts, which have realised that their traditional policy of defending small static reserves – natural ghettoes, their own "phantasy" retreats from the real world – is a dead end, and have begun moving increasingly towards the restoration and creation of big landscapes, that need the minimum of human interference.'

A few comments are in order here: for a start, I can only accept Richard Mabey's view that this is indeed now the policy of the Wildlife Trusts; I do not know. I presume from the wording that Richard approves of this change in conservation policy but, if he does, I cannot quite see how he can reconcile it with his suggestions that we need completely to rethink woodland policy. In that context, he says, 'Much more diverse planting schemes should be tried,' something with which I am again in total agreement.

In any case, surely, the state of this one planet we inhabit is now seen so be so parlous that we have to do both. Biodiversity, the wonderful, complex, ebullient web of life is generally agreed to be one of the most important aspects of the natural world, something that we have to maintain, partly because it is a beautiful and natural mystery, partly because what we understand of it suggests that it is a crucial part of our own life-support system. And, at least in the wonderfully complex countryside of the Highlands and Islands, biodiversity certainly needs those 'small, static reserves' even if that description does not sound very exciting. Take the example I have already given, of the island of Rum. If I were being caustic, I would say that NCC and SNH have been running the island on the 'landscapes' principle, with a concentration on two landscapes – one devoted to trees, the other to deer. (In fact, I would accept that there has probably been a third, that of the high hills.) In the devotion of the one landscape to deer, as I have already made clear, I feel that at least one very special habitat – that of the 'machair' coastal grassland of Kilmory – has been allowed to suffer, and is no longer in 'favourable condition'. It certainly has not been during the last few visits I made there. What that means is that biodiversity, both 'local' (at Kilmory) and 'island' (the whole of Rum) is reduced.

How we should treat the vast sweeps of the Highland landscape is not exactly crystal-clear to me, but I am at least sure that we must not lose sight of the small areas of diversity that they do contain. So much of the country was formerly painstakingly surveyed that we do at least know what and where most of them were, even if some of us wish the initial writing had been more accessible. In the old days, when NCC staff were encouraged to get out of the office, or simply did so, they got to know their patch in detail, and could see any local problems as they emerged. They also then had the freedom to go and talk, regularly, to the landholders and managers. Although the two groups may have been chalk and cheese, may have talked different languages, at least they had the chance to establish, however slowly, some sort of relationship, a basis on which to work. And part of that lay in a recognition from the landlord's side that the NCC staff-member knew the ground, and what was going on in it and on it. SNH staff, however willing and knowledgeable they may be, are now comparatively office-bound, and mostly lack the opportunity to spend time out in the places they are meant to be looking after. Whether that will ever change for the better I do not know, but the gap may be filled, in some lucky places at least, by the presence of an active and knowledgeable Field Club. Assynt, for years, has had one such, and its many useful activities have often been supported by SNH, so good things are still happening in some places.

The question, though, of what to do about the great tracts of countryside with which we are concerned, is still difficult. People expect a lot of trees, and a lot of trees have been planted in some places: a million by NCC/SNH in Rum, and a million by Trees for Life in the Central Highlands. In this case, I would suggest that in future we plant less and diversify much more. But, in any case, a much larger area, because of the presence of peat, will not nourish trees and should definitely not be planted. We should be stricter about this; in a number of places, I have inspected the scooped-up mounds that increasingly disfigure our landscapes in the name of 'planting future woodlands', and a number of them I could quite easily have cut, dried and burnt in the days when I was cutting peat for winter warmth. Mounding like this must surely dry and oxidise the peat, releasing carbon dioxide and methane into the atmosphere. Even if we aim, where we can, at 'the restoration and creation of big landscapes' throughout the Highlands and Islands, I am clear that we must still see and understand the small patches that are different and often full of delight.

There remain, then, the big sweeps of moorland, some with thick heather, some wetter and with much less, but all subject to the types of historic management we have been discussing. (Please note that I am not referring here to the great peatlands of Sutherland and Caithness, nor the smaller, but frequent patches of patterned bog seen elsewhere; rather, I'm discussing the more ordinary, extensive landscape that we who inhabit it just call 'the hill'.) Where there is any peat at all, we should, in my view, not plant – whether you love them or loathe them, the open spaces of the Scottish Highlands and Islands are a defining characteristic. We know now that their present state is at least partly natural, the result of climatic changes impacting on often impervious rocks, and we know that the resultant, acid soils have been further acidified by pollution caused by the outpourings of heavy industry elsewhere. There will be deer passing over them from time to time, and, rather paradoxically, if their population is 'properly' controlled – so that they do not, for instance, threaten the future of any woodland occurring elsewhere in their range – the heather, coarse grasses and sedges may be long enough to shade anything else out. Otherwise, you will see almost no mammals and, normally, few birds, perhaps only meadow-pipits (you can really start to worry if you see none of those). We have established that these moors are vastly less productive than they were only 200 years ago; should we try to return them towards their former condition? If so, how do we do it?

I am intrigued, given the present condition of these expanses, by the possibility of a few small experiments into the effects of what seems always to be called 'remineralization'. I recall, quite a few years ago, passing on my way to Kindrogan in Strathardle, an old, marginal farm, which was said to be experimenting with this process of applying ground-up rock-dust to soils (echoing the effects, thousands of years ago, of the action of glaciers). But I have heard little since. The process is normally considered in the context of agriculture or horti-culture, but as one of its claimed benefits is to 'rebalance soil pH', I do wonder whether it might be worth seeing if it could cancel out the recent increases in acidification in the uplands. Clearly, there are all sorts of potential factors to consider – what type of rock-dust, and how much – and ultimately there may be all sorts of objections. I would, at first, I think, make such experiments in a varied landscape, so if the visual effect of the mineral application was noticeable, it would not stand out too much. I anticipate all kinds of negative reaction to this modest proposal, but I have to point out that in Norway and Sweden, in order to offset the effects of acid rain, they have been liming the freshwater lakes for a number of years (and there are lots of lakes in Sweden). We may have to decide soon whether to emulate this courage and scale of commitment. It is worth looking at the website – remineralize.org – to see what you think.

Eighteen

A DRIVE UP THE
STRATH OF KILDONAN

We start down by the sea in Helmsdale. The place-name interests me because it is Scandinavian (or Norse, if you prefer)
and has survived in popular use despite the fact that there
appears to have been some Gaelic spoken in the area before the
Vikings arrived (maybe around 800–900 AD), and there certainly must have been plenty of Gaelic after the Scandinavian
power declined. The element 'kil' in the valley name Kildonan
indicates a site occupied by monks of the early Celtic Church,
and two saints, Ninian and Donan, are associated with the area.
As a location, it is exactly the sort of place where you might
expect to find evidence of early settlement: the narrow strip of
coastal agricultural land disappears at this point, as the high hills
of the Ord cut it off to the north. Here the wide river flowing
down its fertile strath enters the sea, and a post-glacial beach-
level provides space for settlement. There is room for a reasonable harbour at the river-mouth, which was once guarded
by an old castle. William Daniell painted the scene in 1820, by
which time the work of building the new harbour and planned
village was well underway; all this was to provide employment
in the fishing industry for some, at least, of the numerous folk
who were cleared from the strath. New crofts, on a regular

pattern, were also created on the south side of the river as it approaches Helmsdale; they are still very obvious today.

Somewhat unusually, the Strath of Kildonan is at its most impressive – the hillsides highest – here where the river meets the sea. As we drive upriver, they will become more gentle and lower, the scene widening out before us as we swing north. It is late spring, or early summer, depending on when you think summer actually begins, and there are lambs in the fields, and the gorse is at its brilliant best. The first section of the valley is well-wooded, each tree with its own distinct and special green in the way that marks this beautiful time of year, and we see the occasional white foaming blossom of a gean or the marginally creamier flowers of bird cherry. A cuckoo, too, calls some-where ahead. The river, not exactly high, winds calmly across the flat floor of the strath; there are one or two small islands close to the road, covered in primroses, which, we deduce, stags do not like, as there are three here, quite unworried that we are watching them, eating everything else, constantly and steadily.

We continue gently along the road, past only a few houses and then, after some considerable time, notice a place where there obviously once was a house of some size: there is level grass and some fine trees. This was in fact the site of one of the big lodges along the river, Suisgill, which was burnt down. The name is again Norse and implies a small ravine; a side burn joins the main river close by.

We stop the car and wander to the riverside. Here there are small falls and rapids, with long pools, and trees along the other bank. A high piping announces the presence of the common sandpiper, and we watch two of them on the far stony shore. A flash of gorgeous yellow and a long, wagging tail mean that we also have that truly misnamed bird, the so-called 'grey' wagtail. It is a lovely day and a lovely place.

As the trees thin out, the valley sides become increasingly heather-covered, still the deep brown of winter, rich in the sun, with narrow splashes of rusty red where the bracken grows – but fresh green growth is coming up fast. This hillside is obviously reasonably well drained and quite fertile; there are low walls to be noticed among the heather, and one or two still-imposing archaeological sites. People lived here for a long time, and left many traces of their presence, in structures and in place names. Further up, across the wide glen, there is a mildly baronial grey house, Borrobol, whose name indicates a Viking farm.

But there are traces here of an historical event far removed from the inevitable procession of Gaelic-Pictish-Viking-Norman of the place-names or archaeological sites. In a hollow, by a side burn, a surprisingly large sign reads 'Baile an Or', the 'Town of Gold'. A gold nugget had actually been found in the area in 1818, but more discoveries led to a gold rush in 1869 and a shanty-town sprang up as folk rushed to pan for gold in the burns – which apparently, you may still do today.

We, however, carry on up the road, only stopping a while later when a male hen harrier, long-winged, long-tailed, the 'huge blue bird' of John Clare, crosses the narrow road ahead of us and slants off up the hill. It flies low, rocking slightly as it checks the pale grasses below for mice or small birds. Its blue-grey back and conspicuous white-ringed tail are almost lost for a moment against the blue of distant hills, still streaked with the last snow, soft white in the hazy afternoon. Ahead are huge open spaces, the wide moors and Flow Country of the empty interior of the vast county of Sutherland.

This is, like Glenleraig or Glencalvie, another of those places that makes you ponder. Kildonan was cleared during the years 1813 to 1819, so almost immediately after Glenleraig. After the evictions came the sheep, with the shepherds, then the

keepers and the big lodges, but it remained a somewhat depopulated glen. It so happens that the river, the Helmsdale, is one
of the finest and most prestigious of Highland salmon rivers,
and fishing along it is extremely expensive, giving the estates
with rights to do so, huge value and prestige. The contrast, I
think, between the fate of those who were forced to leave the
strath, and the wealth of the few who come to enjoy its fishing
today, has meant that it has remained a focus for heated debate,
both about the need for land reform and the real potential of
such places. As to the former, I have mentioned the degree
of reform that has allowed communities like those in Eigg,
remote Knoydart and, of course, Assynt (where it all started) to
buy and manage the land as they wish. To enable a mix of types
of landlord, along the lines I have previously mentioned, can
only be a good thing and some are certainly flourishing – but
with a lot of hard work. It is, however, not exactly the sort of
revolution that some people want.

The truth is, sadly, that in some areas, the relationship
between the surrounding estates and the rest of the local population has sometimes (or often) been poor. Where you have
a significantly expensive salmon river owned, managed and
fished by wealthy estates (the proprietors of which are often
absentees), and all those salmon flowing through a small, not
noticeably rich town at its mouth, then one problematical activity is as inevitable as the sunrise tomorrow: poaching. How it is
done, and how it is treated, are old Highland problems.

Much earlier, I mentioned two Highland novelists, the fel-
low-excisemen Neil M. Gunn and Maurice Walsh. Despite
their friendship and their common knowledge of the Highlands,
their books are very different. One of Walsh's best-known tales
is *The Key Above the Door* (W. & R. Chambers, 1926), which is
set in the moorland around Lochindorb. The hero of the story
lives, for much of the year at least, in a cottage on a hillside

overlooking the loch and its old castle, and occupies an ambiguous position in local society (a difficult task, sometimes). The impetus for the entire story is provided by a fishing expedition that is foiled by weather and water-conditions, prompting the three lads to try an illicit method of catching a 'jolly nice fish', which they do – and get caught by the fishing tenant. The local hero, one Tom King, has a 'telepathic twinge. The new tenant might… resent any infringement of his rights. Though we were only playing at poaching, still, poaching we actually were – and using, at that, one of the favourite methods of the experienced and cunning professional.' As the immediate repercussions of this event work out, it emerges in the passing that the tenant and his party had actually caught a nice twelve-pounder in the same unfavourable conditions, also by illegal means.

Neil M. Gunn came from Dunbeath, slightly further up the coast from Helmsdale at the mouth of another river, which also is the title for one of his best works. *Highland River* (The Porpoise Press, 1937) is a much more complex book than Walsh's – it is at least rather less ambiguous in social terms. Its central piece of action is another poaching episode, also at the very beginning of the story. This time, however, it is an epic struggle between an uncompromisingly working-class boy of nine years and a salmon of thirty pounds, a truly big fish. His is one of a series of raids by the boys who lived in the row of small cottages down by the fishing-harbour, on the fish running up the river to spawn. This is all on a smaller scale than at Helmsdale, with fewer people living nearby.

The Laird was a being apart, who visited his mansion house only at intervals. He did not belong to them and they never thought about him; for even their rents were collected by a factor who came for the purpose from his lawyer's office in the county town. The people had an instinctive fear of this factor, and always assumed

their best dress and manners when they went before him to pay
their dues... the only real touch with this curious menace or tyr-
anny of the mansion house was found in the gamekeepers.

Both these accounts give a good impression of the distinctly
ambiguous attitude (on both sides of the social divide) to the
order of poaching described as 'one for the pot', although
at times it was clearly a regular series rather than a one-off.
Certainly, for the poachers, often teenage boys, it was irresistible: 'In all his outings, by himself or with his companions,
the river was an adventure often intense and always secretive.'
Few people, myself included, have felt immune to the attractive combination of the hunting instinct and the delicious fear
of being discovered. It is very hard to generalise here, but I
feel that the most intelligently run estates knew just when to
turn a blind eye, or when to drop a warning in someone's ear.
Some definitely over-reacted and lost, irretrievably, the sense
of fellowship that could exist between the estate and those who
lived on its land.

Commercial poaching, often by groups from 'the city', was
on a different scale and, understandably, a different matter.
Rivers were dynamited, or fish poisoned. Deer were frequently
harried from the roadsides. Although I recognise that such
'lamping' was often cruel, callous and indiscriminate, I must
reluctantly point out that it had one undeniable benefit, which
we have lost: it made the deer very timid, reluctant to linger on
the verges, and the roads much safer than they are now.

Estate owners, their families and staff are, of course, just like
most other members of the human race, in being good, bad or
indifferent, but in areas of small population the reality often
felt more 'feudal' than that, and the question of attitude was
important. Some, on both sides, got it right, and others wrong
– the main problem being that in a social situation like this,

once resentment has surfaced it hangs around for a long time. I would like to hope that such questions are now old-fashioned, redundant, but am not so sure. Some people never seem to recognise that they contribute to making situations worse, particularly, I fear, sometimes the owners and tenants of fishing.

On this very road up the Helmsdale (and on other rivers like the Oykell and Naver), I have several times almost literally been swept aside by a large vehicle, salmon-rods on the bonnet, charging along apparently oblivious to other folk who actually have the temerity to use the same road. And once, further up again, on the road to the north coast, I stopped to make the long walk into the interior and up the twin hills always called the 'Ben Griams'. I had a good day; it began cold, but warmed up, and I enjoyed my exploration of the extensive, puzzling archaeology on the southern face of one hill, and later, relaxing in the warmer afternoon sun on a high alp on the other. I had extensive views over the patterned bogs (and ill-advised forestry) of the Flow Country, and been beguiled by golden plover and dunlin and another harrier, female this time. Tired but contented, I made the long march back along the track to the road and my car. As I approached it, I was perfectly happy until a vehicle came by and a keeper stopped to interrogate me, very officiously, about where I had been and what I had been doing.

It was early summer; there are no rivers up that far, and I was, in any case, carrying neither rod nor gun, nor, obviously, much else in my small rucksack. I suppose that I might have tried to get a few thin grouse with a catapult, but had in fact seen none to poach, even had I the weapon to try to get them with. It was all completely unnecessary, pointless and quite counter-productive. Sadly, some folk never learn.

Nineteen

THE HIGHLAND ESTATE IN THE 21ST CENTURY

Although you might sometimes be forgiven for wondering, today's Highland estates were not ordained by God, nor did they emerge fully formed from the sea. Some were the result of extraordinarily long campaigns of purchase by very rich men. Writing in *Revival of the Land* (Scottish Natural Heritage, 1997), Paul Ramsay explains the chain of property deals that led to the formation of the Ardverikie Estate, of which the tract of land now known as the National Nature Reserve of Creag Meagaidh was once part. In 1869, Sir John Ramsden, who apparently already owned Alvie and Glenfeshie, took over the lease of Ardverikie, on terms that ultimately meant ownership passed to him. He further 'bought the surrounding estates of Ben Alder, Dalwhinnie, Inverpattack, Strathmashie, Glenshero and, in 1877, Moy and Braeroy. (Information from an as-yet unpublished account makes it clear that some of these purchases were facilitated by property that he had bought on the outskirts of Inverness being exchanged with land held by Baillie of Dochfour, requiring a private Act of Parliament.) In 1929, Aberarder was joined to this great complex of deer forests, sheep farms, fishings, grouse moors and woodland operations.' But, sometimes, there were sales, too: 'Loch Laggan Estates sold Moy and Aberarder to Fountain Forestry in 1983.' This was as a result of changes in

Government's view of its own Forestry Commission and 'a glut of Canadian timber' on international markets.

Further north, the vast Sutherland estates extended at one stage right across the enormous county of the same name. They eventually sold Assynt Estate to the Vestey family, who have, through time, sold off pieces of that significant holding, leading to the creation of no fewer than three community-based land-owning ventures within the parish; what are now called the North Assynt Estate (the lands of the Assynt Crofters' Trust), The Assynt Foundation lands (basically the Forests of Glencanisp and Drumrunie), and Little Assynt Estate, owned by the Culag Community Woodland Trust. The Vestey brothers still own quite a lot of land there, and there is also the privately owned Ardvar Estate, while the John Muir Trust owns the adjoining mountain of Quinag. This makes the role of the local Deer Management Group quite challenging at times!

It is vital to note here that when these estates were being built up, they were acquired by men of vast riches, who went on to invest hugely in the property they had bought. Paul Ramsay again: 'Sir John erected forty-five miles of deer fence, thirty-five miles of sheep fence, and built forty miles of roads. For fifteen years he planted one million trees a year.' It is worth reading those few sentences again, I think – they reveal so much. They highlight that big houses, stables and cottages were not the only things that these proprietors spent money on. They reveal how compartmentalised the Highland landscape was becoming. They explain, perhaps, the occasionally rather fanatical attitude of some of the current owners and, almost more important than all the rest put together, they reveal the extraordinary amount of maintenance work that the original proprietors and builders bequeathed to their descendants – without, of course, knowing how different economic conditions would be well over 100 years later. Virtually all these grand estates were originally highly subsidised by wealth-creating activities elsewhere, and all prospective purchasers of such estates today ought to be made aware of the real necessity of such external sources of wealth. That fine new lodges are still being built indicates that this is at least sometimes the case; I think of the lovely, newish house just above Milton in Strath Conon (and Scardroy Lodge at the very end of the public road there has doubled in size since I first knew it), Eilean Aigas and Old Corrour to which I have already referred, and there were rumours some years ago that a lodge in Sutherland was acquiring a ballroom.

The fact is that all these estates were originally expensive luxuries, and that is how they should be regarded today, most certainly not as sources of wealth. Sadly, you may see all over the Highlands, if you know where to look, the results of inadequate resourcing: poorly maintained estate buildings and cottages; badly thought-out and unmanaged forestry projects; and the occasional hare-brained idea like holding mid-winter wedding receptions in remote, under-staffed, freezing lodges. In recent years, wind-farms have come along just in time to rescue quite a few of them but, again, it only needs a couple of changes in Government policy and the wind-farms will be as redundant as some of the plantations scattered across our landscapes. It is in many ways, I think, a great shame that there is still a fashion for acquiring Scottish estates, as the prices are in fact driven by that fashion, and do not reflect the uncomfortable fact that they are based neither on the limited opportunities to *make* money from them, nor the almost unlimited opportunities to *spend* money on them. Often enough, it is the landscape that suffers in the long run.

I referred earlier to the occasionally rather fanatical attitudes of some landowners. In many cases it originated in the desire to protect from disturbance all the sporting activities on their land, but it suits a country with an established 'Right to Roam' rather badly. When I was a boy, the Letterewe Estate, on the north side of Loch Maree, was a byword for problems, as the owner regarded it as an entirely private domain. I did myself know a proprietor who admitted that the public had the right to drive along the road up a particular glen, part of which he owned, but maintained that they had no right at all to stop and get out of their cars – even if it were just to stand and look around. Once, when spending a few days away from home, I politely phoned one estate office to ask whether there might be a day when it would be possible for me to climb the very fine mountain that they owned, without disturbing any sporting activity. The reply was one word: 'No.' I then phoned a neighbouring estate, who owned a neighbouring mountain, to ask the same question: the reply was charming, appreciative and helpful. Neither of them knew at the time that I was a journalist – they did later. At least nobody I ever heard of followed the example of Compton Mackenzie's Ben Nevis, who locked some hikers overnight in a dungeon. Although I have no doubt that problems remain, the legal position now is at least reasonably clear.

Access often brings with it tracks, like the fine stalkers' paths known to so many walkers. The earlier ones were generally just wide enough for a pony but, through time, they became wide enough for a Land Rover and, given the climate of the Scottish Highlands, maintenance became a significant issue. There used to be, officially at least, controls on the number of such tracks, but in recent years they have proliferated, and added to their number have been tracks to forestry schemes, small hydro projects, the new pylons and wind-farms. In some ways I feel that these are actually preferable to the lines created by all-terrain vehicles (ATVs) repeatedly following the same route over the hills and bogs, leading eventually to significant erosion. And if we are arguing constantly for control of deer numbers, particularly the stalking of hinds (crucial in controlling the population) in the short winter days, it seems hard to argue against the tracks that make the task a little bit easier. I had a friend, a keeper, who lives in pain with a bad back that is the result of years of dragging deer out over the rough and wet Highland terrain, often in the foulest of conditions. There must be many like him.

Given the frequent references to forestry, sometimes in completely inappropriate places like the Flow Country, given the tracks, pylons and wind-farms, as well as the much older but far-reaching hydro projects, it would be most revealing to see them all mapped. It would certainly show how much genuinely wild country actually remains in this supposedly wild land, and mapping fences both for sheep and deer would enormously reduce that area again. You could argue, of course, that it might not be that different from a map of the Highlands before the Clearances when, as we have seen, for instance, much of the Assynt hinterland was populated. The difference is that this map would show the location of some of the components of life in the 21st-century Highlands – but with no one actually living there around them.

I have worked with a few estates, both large and small, and observed many others. Some co-exist pretty well with the communities around them, others never quite manage it – or do not care, which is most regrettable. The presence of a resident factor, especially when the owners are absentees, can be a useful bridge, although it is in itself a demanding role. Doing without a local factor is often a false economy in the long run. It must be admitted, however, that even the newer, community-owned estates do not always find it easy to get the backing of the entire community they are trying to represent. Such estates often do manage to engage the interest, enthusiasm and knowledge of at least some members of that community, leading to a wave of creative energy and many good projects initiated, sometimes with a huge voluntary input. However, in small communities there are almost always two problems. One is sustaining that initial enthusiasm into the future, and the other is finding adequate sources of income. Magic, instant solutions to these problems have been rather few, and a number of estates have instead ended up, against their initial instincts perhaps, realising their potential as traditional sporting estates.

This actually makes a lot of sense. As I have said, the Highland sporting estate is not exactly God-given, nor is it a cash cow, but it does seem to represent a reasonable way of earning some money for at least as long as there are rich people around who want to experience this way of life. Estates, particularly those subsidised on a significant scale from outwith the area, do bring cash into the local economy, but I remain convinced that the potential, for instance, from sales of venison is, rather oddly, far from being fully realised. I know that the measures of land reform which have taken place are not enough to satisfy a number of people, but they have achieved positive results and given many local people something substantial and worthwhile to engage with. As a society, we don't really do revolutions, and I think it is reasonable to suggest that this is about as far as it will go, although minor improvements will, I hope, emerge with time.

And, being perhaps rather cynical and certainly pragmatic, I offer the following (admittedly not very lofty) justification for the future of the sporting estate: if its continuing existence can persuade people to come to the Highlands and Islands and to pay significant amounts of money to help reduce the population of a grazing animal, now so numerous as to be a threat to the future of most of our native woodlands, then I am all for it. I have been accused of being 'against deer'; this is not true, but increased numbers of any creature can turn it into a pest. Ironically, the Victorian sporting culture has done just that.

Twenty

A DRIVE AROUND ROUSAY

If you happen to be in the Strath of Kildonan and heading for Orkney, as I so often have been, the simplest thing is to continue driving north. The route lies through a small part of the Flow Country, through Forsinard, and then down a smaller river, the Halladale, to the coast. Here we turn to the right and head east, through farms and small villages – and past the Dounreay Nuclear Power Station, now being slowly decommissioned. At one point the road twists above the meander of a river backed by a large plantation, which is mostly sycamore; this hides the handsome Forss House, now a hotel. Further on, we reach the outskirts of Thurso, one of the two main towns of this northeastern county of Caithness.

Thurso is a dignified, planned town, laid out in the 19th century, with broad streets and an ornamental garden in Sir John's Square, named after Sir John Sinclair of Ulbster, who pioneered many agricultural reforms in Caithness. We have already heard of him, as he it was who introduced the sheep to Caithness in 1792, ten years after it first appeared in Glengarry. As I've described in *North and West*, his experiment was obviously entirely successful, 'but while plenty of landowners were happy to follow his example in introducing sheep to the glens, few, it appeared, were prepared to listen to his advice on its implementation. It was his view that tenants should, in essence, form sheep-rearing co-operatives and purchase small flocks, for which they would hire shepherds, paying rent partly in kind.' This must be one of the most significant 'what-if' moments in Highland history: if the overwhelming majority of landowners had followed his advice, the subsequent history of places like Kildonan would have been very different. I imagine that there might well still have been some emigration from the North, perhaps on a significant scale, but the drastic emptying of the glens need not have happened, and much of the Highlands would look rather different.

Sadly, we cannot rewrite history, and we are in any case not visiting Thurso. We turn sharp left, under the imposing Scrabster House, white-harled, towered and turreted, a good Victorian building. I see that the RCAHMS (Royal Commission on the Ancient and Historical Monuments of Scotland) website states that 'Scrabster House is a 19th-century mansion of no architectural significance', a description that does little justice to its strong presence overlooking the port, where we take the ferry to Orkney.

This approach to the isles must rank as the finest such experience in the whole of Britain. The first part, across the wider section of the Pentland Firth, is perhaps almost ordinary, and certainly often uneventful, despite the fearsome reputation of this piece of water. Slowly, we approach the cliffs of Hoy (the 'high island'), and they are remarkable, partly simply for their height, which slowly increases as we progress under them, then pass the famous Old Man of Hoy, to culminate in St John's Head, towering over 350 metres above us. More wonderful to me than the sheer height of the cliffs is their deep and varied colouring. Where we first see them, they tend to be a warm-ish brown, sometimes ochre, but after the single break for the wide valley and beach of Rackwick, they become redder, and along the highest section, by the Old Man, they are a deep red, splashed with the vivid green of luxuriant vegetation growing on the horizontal ledges.

Then the ferry turns into a wide channel where a strong current is often visible; the corries and peaks of the Hoy Hills are to the right, while ahead a gentler landscape beckons, flowing shapes and soft colours. This is Mainland Orkney, the largest island in the archipelago. At this point, we suddenly find that we are making a hard turn towards the west, into a sheltered inlet, backed by a low hill above a small, intricate huddle of simple, grey-harled houses and piers; this is Stromness, where we leave the ferry.

We are heading for another island, and we cross the West Mainland, the largest body of land in the islands. There is a lot of freshwater, two large lochs in particular appear very soon after we have left the small port. These, the Lochs of Stenness and Harray, lie in wide, smooth basins of rich agricultural land, rimmed by smooth heather hills. This is a land of big Victorian fields; the fashion for agricultural improvement reached here around 1850, and draining permitted the reclamation of some of the flatter, boggier ground. Thankfully, some of it remains and important wetlands are a significant component in the mosaic of habitats here. These islands are good for birds, which appear to co-exist well with the farmers' management of the rich grassland; I see evidence of chemical weedkillers very rarely, which must be an important, beneficial factor. Because the ground under the heather of the hills is basically fertile, large areas of it were converted to pasture at the same time but, again fortunately, much remains, and there are no longer any incentives for such change. Some older buildings still stand, but there are few traces of the earlier patterns of occupation and working.

The remarkable density of rural settlement is noticeable, as are the relics from much older times. We pass a small but obvious chambered tomb, on a narrow peninsula just after the outflow from the Loch of Stenness and later, in the scattered community of the same name, in the distance across the water, the great stones of the Ring of Brodgar stand, clear if the light is good, but always mysterious. Then the fewer, taller Stones of Stenness and, still on the left, a smaller stone in a field, followed by the imposing mound of Maeshowe. This fertile land has a long history.

If we were intending to visit Maeshowe (it is probably the finest chambered tomb in Western Europe), we would have to park on the other side of the road beside what was, very obviously, an important water-powered mill. It now serves as a visitor centre for Historic Scotland (which owns and manages Maeshowe). The website records that 'it was built in 1884–5 by Colonel Balfour of Shapinsay to serve the local tenant farmers'. There are many such mills in Orkney and Caithness, testament again to the Victorian reorganisation of local agriculture.

Shortly after this, the road dips slightly; there is a remaining patch of heathland, then a junction, then more big fields with a large establishment coming into view on the left. This is Binscarth, with quite a lot of trees, almost the first we have seen on the island. The leading edge of the extensive planting, mostly of sycamore at least along the exposed fringes, is very visibly wind-pruned – in Orkney, you don't plant shelter-belts, you plant trees in the sheltered places, of which there are rather few. It is a big farm; the farm square has nice pyramidal roofs on its corner 'towers', and the farmhouse is solid and dignified. The mansion of 1850 is higher up, above the long plantation leading down the valley almost to a small inlet of the sea. The woodland was extended in recent years, and you may walk through it; in spring it is full of bluebells (the Spanish ones, which do well here) and carpeted by a starry pink-white flower, the pink purslane, again an exotic but one which flourishes in these damp northern plantations, and gives them real enchantment. Such places give important shelter to small birds as well as providing sites for large, noisy rookeries, are much used by migrants, and make a refuge from the winds for visitor and resident alike.

Finstown, just beyond here, is one of the few oldish villages, benefitting from a fair degree of shelter; it has lovely gardens and trees. Our road is to the left, northwards, through farmland backed by hills, to the terminal for the ferry to Rousay. But again, there are unreclaimed areas, places dark with heather, once used for cutting peat. I sometimes stop along a by-road here, and wait quietly in a passing-place, watching the level expanse all around. There are large mounds of willow, maybe only six feet in height, but several times that in circumference; perhaps this is what the ancient Orkney scrub woodland was actually like, with some birch, alder and aspen? Much is heather, but areas of deep green vegetation are meadowsweet, which will be a delight in a few weeks' time, with flowers like cream foam and a heavy scent. If you listen, in the distance there is curlew-music, and one may do its display-flight close by. Sometimes a harrier will pass, and often there are short-eared owls, hunting by day just like the harriers, and for the same prey. One may drop suddenly into the heather and remain hidden for a while, sometimes another will land on a fence-post and turn to watch us, its 'cattie-face' (the local name) and great glowing eyes powerful, mesmerising.

Folk are planting some new woods in this relatively sheltered part of Mainland Orkney, and soon its patchwork scenery may be even more diverse. We reach a rise, from which we have a fine view northwards over the sea and scattered isles; the largest of these – a long, dark ridge running west – is Rousay and our destination. The ferry terminal of Tingwall is small, a ramp and a pier, lobster-pots and cars, a small office with a friendly face, the vital loos, and people wandering in all directions. Soon

the ferry itself – a landing-craft type of vessel, somewhat awkward of access for the car-driver – appears and shortly after we
are on the narrow, breezy passenger-deck, heading through
the fulmars and eider ducks, past the seals hauled out on the
dark slabs. To our west, we see yet another plantation, and the
tower of another big house, that of Woodwick. It is probably slightly later, but is very much in the Victorian style, with
beautiful grounds. We are crossing the shallow waters of the
Sound of Eynhallow, on our way to the island of Rousay, all
very romantic!

After a while, the low-lying island of Wyre appears on our
right; there were always herons along this shore when I lived
in Orkney many years ago, but they have, mysteriously, disappeared. We do, however, see seals resting on one of the low
skerries when the tide is right, and greylag geese, whose numbers are expanding all over the north of Scotland, are nearly
always on the opposite Rousay shore. As we approach the small
settlement and pier of Brinyan, we have a splendid view of the
house of Trumland (built in 1873), its extensive policy woodlands and large farm. Part of the big range of buildings belonging to the latter has been somewhat ruinous in recent years, but
an exciting restoration of one section indicates, I hope, how
it may all eventually appear. Such buildings are expensive to
maintain, especially in the windy climate of Orkney.

Once landed, we make our way between the few houses
of Brinyan, a settlement that hardly existed before the ferry
terminal was located here. The population was formerly rather
scattered, the island being divided into districts; at one stage,
I imagine, each must have had its own church and possibly its
own school. The island did for long look depopulated, especially in comparison with the West Mainland, but new houses
have appeared in recent years; some around Brinyan with
attractive, wooded gardens. As we reach the head of the brae,

and the road around the island, Trumland looms before us, but as we will return this way, too, we will leave much discussion of it until later. Some reference to the man who built it must, however, be made at this stage, because General Burroughs, always known (not very affectionately) as 'the Little General', was the man most responsible for the depopulated appearance of Rousay. Of all the islands in Orkney, next to Hoy, Rousay is the most Highland in appearance, with central heather-covered hills and a couple of lochs. Like much of the Highlands, it suffered from Clearances, and there is plenty of evidence for this era as we go around on the single-track road.

That road itself almost forms the boundary between the farmed ground, with its big rectangular fields, and the rough hill. There are a few scattered cottages; one rejoices still in the name of 'Bellona', the name of Burroughs' favourite warhorse. There are wonderful views of two small islands, the first of which we passed on the ferry. Both are gentle in scenery, farming country but perhaps rather marginal in population; today in the sun, they lie like jewels in an enamelled sea, but life in small islands cannot always be idyllic. Both have monuments from an ancient past; the small Norse castle and chapel on Wyre lie low and are not easy to see, but the tall tower of the church of St Magnus on Egilsay is very conspicuous. This group of small isles was home for a while to one of Orkney's foremost literary figures, the poet Edwin Muir, who remembered, as a boy, seeing Burroughs walking around his estate and the demands he made on those he permitted to remain. Memories of Orkney sustained Edwin Muir as a youth when his family moved away; four of them died in quick succession and for some years he coped with a number of unpleasant jobs in industrial Glasgow.

The next district is that of Sourin, where a broad agricultural valley leads down from the hills to the sea; a 19th-century mill indicates the productivity of these big fields at that time. The community school has been extended, another indication of the improving fortunes of the island, and the cages of a salmon farm provide one of the reasons for that increased prosperity. Having crossed the burn, the straight road rises quite steeply, and on the right one of the most remarkable natural features of Rousay becomes very visible. This is a series of terraces, alternating hard and soft layers of sandstone, shaped by the huge erosive forces of the Ice Age. Neat cottages sit comfortably on the flat shelves, but beyond them, some are abandoned, rusty roofs of corrugated iron bright in the sun. Big fields again lie between our ascending road and the distant rise of Faraclett Head; there are significant ancient monuments along the low line of crags – 'hammars', they are called in Orkney. We stop at the very highest point of the road to admire the huge view, a great arc of sea and islands. The land falls away steeply beneath us to the dark waters of Saviskaill Bay, but further along the shore, small patches are shallow and sandy, a brilliant turquoise.

The lower ground ahead is that of another district, Wasbister (always called 'Wester'), with rich fields grouped around a small loch whose narrow outflow once drove another mill. It is worth the detour down to the bay – there are nearly always seals on the shore and small waders on the patch of sand. Above the farms are smaller cottages, some ruined; on more marginal land, there are crofts where Burroughs permitted some evicted tenants to remain. Many of these collapsing vernacular buildings show the use of local flagstone in wall and roof. I have frequently been told that Burroughs refused permission to use small quarries on Rousay to obtain such flags for building or repair, and they had to be taken from smaller islets, reachable only in rowing boats, access made even more problematic by winds and fierce tidal currents. As we climb out of Wester, the road is soon edged by the well-built dykes of the landowner's sheep farm. We often see short-eared owls on the hill above the road, but the natural tendency is to take in the view on the other side, below us, down to the open ocean.

Over the fine wall, and across the remains of the much older hill-dyke of turf and stone, grassy slopes sweep down to the endless sea. This is a very broad, gentle valley – Quandale or Quendale, depending on your source. As you look down it, you can see some traces of walls and the remains of one upstanding, possibly very old house. William P. L. Thomson, the modern historian of Orkney and author of the exhaustive *New History of Orkney* (Mercat Press, 1987), records that eighty people were evicted from here and replaced by one shepherd. He adds that one James Leonard of Digro was evicted 'for giving evidence to a Royal Commission'. In fact, General Burroughs 'refused to give an assurance that there would be no victimisation of those who gave evidence to the [Napier] Commission [of 1883–84]... and there was, subsequently, a very public ten-year war of attrition between Burroughs and his crofting tenants'. The Commission was mostly made up of landlords, but the findings of its investigations into conditions on the land led in 1886 to the Crofters' Act, 'the main provisions of which protected crofters from eviction and arbitrary rack-renting. Not only were crofters given security of tenure, but they might assign their croft to a member of the family or other successor.' This finally brought some stability to a section of the population of the Highlands and Islands whose lives had been in a state of flux throughout the long period during which the great estates were established; the full story has been told by many writers, most notably James Hunter.

Leaving Quendale, we turn a corner with views across to Costa Head on Mainland, and find ourselves heading somewhat inland, above a wide channel divided by the low island of Eynhallow, the 'Holy Island'. It was so named, perhaps, because of the small Norse monastery on its far side. The very edge of the Sound, far below us, is lined with fine monuments from several periods, the oldest being the immense tomb of Midhowe, which is around 5,500 years old. Like the neighbouring broch from the Iron Age, it and many other island sites were excavated by Walter Grant, a later laird. Among the buildings on the shore (and resting on earlier structures) are the remains of the old farms of Brough and of Skaill. Although folk may have lingered in some of the houses, their lands became part of the big fields of the impressive sheep farm, which run right up to our road. Further on, the farmhouse, its steading and other outbuildings may be seen down the hill, close to the walled plantation that surrounds Westness House. An older house, it was somewhat remodelled by Burroughs when he inherited the island, but was apparently not considered grand enough, which was why he commissioned the building of Trumland further along the coast.

Heading in that direction, we pass through the next district of Frotoft, attractive with its backdrop of terraced hill and scattered fuschia bushes. There is another fine farm here, and some renovated cottages, one with a standing stone at an old, rounded gable. More chambered tombs look down on the scene and, yet further on, we can see an obvious, but unexcavated mound beside the sea, another of the brochs along the shore. Around the next corner or two, and a small mound, high above us, marks the unique, tiny, two-storeyed tomb of Taversoe Tuick, where it was once proposed to place a garden seat so that the view over sea and isles might be enjoyed in comfort.

We are now back at the edge of the extensive policies of Trumland House. Set in a wide and shallow valley, looking roughly eastwards and with a valuable degree of protection from all westerly winds, Trumland is a rather tall and somewhat gaunt house, designed by David Bryce, an architect from

Edinburgh. He apparently promised General Burroughs that it would cost '£3,000... or less', but the final bill was £10,374. It is sometimes said that this left Burroughs with debts that may have caused his avaricious behaviour towards the Rousay crofters, but it was presumably also he who continued with the layout of the policies and plantations, the formal garden, the long drive and gate-lodge, let alone the substantial farm, although Walter Grant certainly spent money on the place in his turn. As far as I have been able to discover, the latter was regarded as a generous laird (the writer Eric Linklater certainly thought so), and his occupation seems to have been one of the happiest periods in the existence of that somewhat unfortunate house.

Like many other such houses, Trumland has suffered from at least one catastrophic fire. One certainly occurred since I first went there; after a long period of neglect, the house was being thoroughly restored and work was finishing on the roof when it caught fire and was substantially damaged. The exterior has since once again been restored, while a great deal has been achieved in the garden and policies, and I understand that work has begun on the interior. It was certainly a very sad place when it was all slowly crumbling and, being so conspicuous in its commanding position, seemed to cast a gloom over that corner of the island.

Ardverikie, on Loch Laggan, is another great house that has arisen from the ashes. The building we see now is not the one that Queen Victoria stayed in, nor the one built to replace it. The Estate website makes clear that the original house burnt down in 1871, and that Sir John Ramsden immediately made plans to replace it. Just as this new building was being completed, in October 1873, it burnt down in its turn, apparently due to 'hot coals being left in a fire-bucket in one of the bedrooms'. Reconstruction began again at once on a rather larger scale and produced the building we see today. In

1915, a fire ravaged much of the Victorian end of Dunrobin Castle, and apparently might well have destroyed most of the huge building, had not hundreds of sailors arrived from vessels lying off the coast to assist in fighting the flames. At the time, the castle was acting as a naval hospital; it has since also been a private school. Dunrobin has a very long history, incorporating a 13th-century tower within its palatial grandeur, while Ardverikie and Trumland are much younger, but all three have come through bad and good times.

Twenty-one

TRANSFORMED LANDS

Another day, another island. Shapinsay is not precisely flat, but low and gently undulating and very agricultural. A glance at the map reveals that the human imprint on the land is remarkably regular: the public roads running fairly straight, and the farm roads leading off them at ninety degrees. William Thomson describes this in greater detail in his *New History of Orkney*, with reference to the Balfour Estate, which borrowed some £6,000 from Government in 1846 for the purpose of drainage and land improvement: 'David Balfour aimed at nothing less than the comprehensive development of the whole island. Marcus Calder, his bagpipe-playing factor, superimposed a grid of ten-acre squares whose straight-line boundaries ran for three miles or more and paid no regard to existing arable land. It was a grid which Balfour was reluctant to modify even when the lie of the land required exceptionally deep ditches.' Maps in this text show the scale of modification, into which the farm roads all, of course, fit. 'It was par excellence the landscape of the big estate.' All this is easy to read or write, but, despite the fact that the eventual outcome was one of improvement and increased prosperity, it must have entailed a long period of real disruption. Something, too, must have been lost along the way; sadly, it seems there was no Orcadian John Clare to tell us what it was.

The gentle landscape of this island is dominated by the bold mass of Balfour Castle, seen from the south against its large plantation. As you walk up the drive, you have to stop to drink in the scale of the building and its complexity. As at Aigas, there lurks here an earlier, much more modest house (called Cliffdale); there is a service wing towards the north and a high domestic block, which catches all the available sun. Balfour was begun in 1847, and was one of David Bryce's earliest country houses. As in the later Trumland, he provided the public rooms with large windows to get the most of the wide views and the Orkney light. Here, too, the drawing room was on a corner, which helps, and, just like Aigas, led to the garden via a conservatory (sadly, the one at Aigas does not survive). Externally, the building is more elaborate than Trumland, with horizontal string-courses, bold windows, corbelling, several crow-step gables and, of course, turrets square and round, and a tower. It is very large and very impressive, a clear statement of Victorian wealth and confidence.

Balfour has been fortunate in its subsequent custodians, and the interior survives in good condition, with some of its original furnishings and all of its original atmosphere. The splendid drawing room is literally the highlight of a tour of the interior, as it contrasts dramatically with the dark opulence of the other public rooms. Lots of details survive, including the metal stag-heads, which were for the gas lighting.

Many Victorian lairds loved to incorporate the latest technology: Kinloch on another, very different island had a splendid scheme for generating hydro-electricity, as well as an internal telephone system and sophisticated ventilation. But things had to look in keeping: the gasometer for Balfour Castle and village, like the big house, had battlements. (There is also an imposing mill for handling the produce from all the improved farms.) Balfour is early in the sequence of building these astonishing houses. The later, rather more modest Trumland cost over £10,000 in 1873. Kinloch must have been finished around 1908, and is said to have cost £250,000, apparently £15 million in today's terms – by coincidence the price at which Eilean Aigas was for sale a couple of years ago. Castles in the mist did not, and do not, come cheap.

In this book, we have worked our way around the North and Central Highlands, touching the Hebrides and Orkney, with reference to places elsewhere. We have thought about the landscape the Victorians found there, and the extensive changes that they made. We have seen their impact on the hill and moorland, the way they changed the woodlands and the fields, the way they moved groups of people out of their way and relocated settlements.

They altered the rivers, and laid out large pleasure-grounds for themselves, centred on the extraordinary proliferation of big, splendid, new houses. They invested money on an immense scale, offered employment to those who were fortunate enough still to be living in their native land, and left huge problems of maintenance to their successors, along with a degree of social tension that may still at times be felt.

I have not written much about the Clearances, because many others have and I have nothing to add to what they have said, often after detailed study. Nothing will alter the fact that they are a seriously disturbing part of Highland and Island history. It can and should be admitted that some degree of fundamental change was inevitable; the growth of the population followed by the Potato Famine alone would have ensured that, but the manner in which those changes were implemented cannot ever be forgotten. It gives me a feeling of unreality that they were happening somewhere in the background throughout almost the entire period I have covered. The pleasure-grounds, the big houses and the sporting estate seem like a stage set; the real human drama was taking place throughout the play but behind the scenes. Ironically, the changes in land use that the Victorians initiated in the uplands seem to be proving in the long run rather less sustainable than the practices they swept away. But change of some kind would have come, and it would probably not have prevented the subsequent waves of depopulation.

The legacy of these Victorians is obviously complex: they shaped our farmland, many of our villages and towns, and provided an infrastructure of roads, railways, bridges and sewers that, effectively, we still use today. In the uplands, in their ruthless pursuit of any creature that might upset their sport, 'they set about a major modification of the natural world', according to Chris Smout in his SNH paper, and very nearly achieved their goal. It is the most painful of ironies to me that without this wholesale destruction we would know less about the landscape they inherited, and which we have lost. One significant cause of the greatly decreased productivity of our hills and moors must be the importance they attached to the stalking of the red deer, and the compartmentalisation of the countryside that stemmed from it. Grouse shooting, too, continues to impact on the landscape and reduce biodiversity.

Clearly, the sporting estate remains and, it appears, will remain – although governments may continue to identify alternative schemes of ownership and wider opportunities. None of this will obscure the reality that there are few opportunities to make significant money in the hills and moors of the Highlands and Islands, and country sports are among those few. That most certainly does not mean that the status quo, as far as

land management is concerned, can simply be allowed to continue unchallenged and unchanged. The sad state to which our
uncontrollably proliferating and destructive species has reduced
its only, home planet makes that imperative (see Epilogue and
Appendix I).

Zealots may want to initiate revolutions, but should be very
wary; this is exactly what the Victorians did. Dreamers may talk
enticingly of 'rewilding', but need to learn and accept realities;
the concept is in any case almost entirely elitist, as wandering
in a wild landscape will never be an experience either desired
by, or available to, the increasing millions in this world whose
ambitions and limitations are almost entirely urban. What we
urgently require is the passionate pragmatist who accepts the
limitations of where we are and where we can go from here,
but can elicit the support of the as yet uninvolved majority,
without whom we are truly lost.

In conclusion, I offer this mild anti-climax: the Victorians
transformed the face of the Highlands and Islands and, in the
process, erected many monuments to themselves. It seems to
me that we remain uncertain how to react to those monuments; on a small scale, there are the regular demands to topple
the first Duke of Sutherland from his high pedestal above
Golspie, and the regular response from around the area that he
is a local landmark and that folk would rather leave him where
he is. We do not seem to know yet quite how to react to all
these arboretums and castellated houses, and we clearly do not
realise the scale and quality of the architectural heritage that
they contribute to the face of our country. The throwaway line
from RCAHMS about Scrabster House – 'of no architectural
significance' – makes this all too clear.

It ought to be obvious that we do not have to endorse the
character and record of every builder of every historic property
in the land in order to be able to enjoy its appearance or the

contribution it makes to the wider landscape. If we did, historic monuments would get very few visitors; battlefields, for instance, would be entirely deserted. History has been; we cannot rewrite it, however passionately we would wish to. We should, surely, accept the evidence for the changes it has brought, and derive from them what rational enjoyment we can.

THE HIGHLANDS IN AN AGE OF CHANGE

It must be clear that the Victorians transformed the Highlands and Islands, and are responsible for much of what we can see there today. They have left us a complex legacy, of good things and bad, which is what you might expect from any group of humans at any particular period. However, we have not entered into just 'any particular period', but into a phase that many of us believe to be both crucial and dangerous. Many of the Victorians who created the large estates made their millions in the early Industrial Revolution, but they died long before the repercussions of that period could be assessed – at least in terms of the environment of the entire planet.

We can now confidently state that there are no parts of the planet which have escaped from the pollution arising out of industrial development, in particular the dependence on fossil fuels and the overwhelming need to mine for minerals. We have, without any doubt, modified the atmosphere that surrounds the Earth, and changed the chemistry of its great, enfolding oceans. Between them, the atmosphere and the oceans are crucial for life on the planet, and drive the weather systems that affect us all. Whether we have merely caused a succession of the hottest years ever recorded, or have been watching a process of fundamental climate change hardly matters; those of us who have lived for a reasonably long time have seen the natural world change during those years, and the demands made on it by our crazily escalating population increase enormously.

It is true that there are some (but now increasingly few) desperately wedded to the status quo (which got us where we are today and made their lives very comfortable) who deny all this. They clutch at straws blowing in the ever-hotter wind, fasten desperately on the occasional human error and miscalculation, and, worst of all, have no 'Plan B'. If (and there is a good chance of it) they are wrong, it will be they who have significantly helped fuck up the lives of our children and their children. It is high time that we ceased to talk about that remote, impersonal thing, 'the Environment' (even in capital letters), and talked instead, and constantly, daily, as a matter of real urgency, about the Earth, this one, home, planet that sustains us now – just about.

With any luck, some of you may agree with all this. But what, in our fast and complex, often struggling, daily lives can we in the Highlands and Islands do about it? At the personal level, there are the obvious ideas, talked about for quite a while now, not yet enough implemented: improve the house insulation, use a 'greener' source of fuel, drive a less-polluting car and less often, buy locally, grow your own vegetables... you know the sort of thing. (For information on these and other possibilities, investigate the Transition Towns initiative; in the Highlands and Islands, Transition Black Isle is leading the way forward). But, other than those good things, what else?

Carbon sequestration is crucial, and we know that the deep peats of the Highlands and Islands are large, important reserves of carbon. They must be maintained with real vigilance and dedication. If in good health, they will be slowly growing, storing carbon away and out of the atmosphere. We must not let them be eroded by sharp hooves, nor by the crude forestry practice of mounding. These are probably our greatest dangers, but the location of wind-farms and access tracks needs to be watched carefully. Trees should only be planted where they have a good chance of growing well.

Maintaining healthy woods allows for carbon-neutral domestic heating, if they are sustainably used as they were in the past, or for more carbon sequestration if they are left simply to grow and regenerate. They need room for manoeuvre, must not be hemmed in, nor further eroded for house-sites. In general, where we are planting, we should plant far smaller woods and do it much better.

Biodiversity, the wonderful, unimaginably complex web of life, has to be maintained at all levels, from your garden to across Sutherland. We have lost a lot in recent years and we have to look to see what we may restore. This will need careful thought, and I think, inevitably, relevant environmental priorities at both the landscape and the small reserve level. We need both. Woods must be significantly more diverse in species, both for biodiversity, interest, and a degree of protection against future exotic pests. Priorities will have to be rethought, a few old ideas abandoned, which some will find painful. If, for instance, there exists an animal that looks like a Scottish wildcat, living where Scottish wildcats should, eating what Scottish wildcats do, then it is playing its ecological part, whatever its DNA – don't spend money on it! (Where there are, for any reason, captive wildcats, of course it makes sense for their progeny to be released into the wild – that is another matter). Beavers should be encouraged, as they do not appear to have blocked the flow of the Tay nor eaten any salmon, and they increase biodiversity where they flourish. Rivers should be much better looked after by those who own the fishing, with trees and luxuriant vegetation restored to much of their banks. Personally, I believe that this needs to become a legal requirement.

Somehow, we need to find ways to encourage the return of small-scale cultivation in the glens and on the crofts; it adds greatly to the visible wealth of life. Livestock can assist in the promotion of biodiversity (whatever George Monbiot thinks), but somehow we need to get them moving around. Nothing has a greater adverse impact on the ground than a group of cattle that are regularly fed in the same spot, and few folk seem to notice that Highland Cattle will regularly eat trees more thoroughly than ever did a sheep, or even a flock of them. Some romantics may dream of herd boys and girls moving cattle over the idyllic Assynt landscape all summer, but the reality is that it will almost certainly never happen. Other ways must be found. Innovators often look backwards, forwards and sideways to achieve beneficial results. But lasting solutions are based on practicalities, an acceptance of limits imposed by nature, and a deep and genuine knowledge of what is there on the ground.

Looking very carefully at what we have on the ground in many places will be critical; in the context of native woodland, it may be that a very detailed look at woods like the one I visited above Loch Morlich (on the way up to the Pass of Ryvoan) will be instructive. It certainly looks 'on the surface' as if it should be fairly rich in overall biodiversity. Another that is repaying comprehensive study (and where Trees for Life have a crucial role to play) is Dundreggan. According to their website (February 2015), Trees for Life are making strong, and apparently rather contradictory claims for their '10,000-acre flagship forest restoration project' in beautiful Glen Moriston. They say that it has 'substantial areas of ancient woodlands, including remnants of the original Caledonian Forest, superb birch-juniper woodlands and the largest expanse of dwarf birch in Scotland'. Crucially, 'the richness and diversity of wildlife at Dundreggan is astonishing. Over 3,000 species have been discovered, with some found nowhere else in the UK. Sadly, having been previously managed as a sporting estate, much of Dundreggan is in poor condition'. If you overlook the hype, and if both the latter statements are true, Dundreggan should have critical lessons for us; it is vital that we know exactly what they are.

Chris Smout reminds us in *Nature Contested* that even with the mixed legacy from the period during which the sporting estate was at its height, and with the fall-out from industrial processes all over the world, these hills and moors still retain something special:

> *The transformed uplands have had a long time to establish their own distinctive ecosystems, adapted to a nutrient-poor environment, and these, too, are highly valued. One quarter of all the British invertebrates, for instance, are found on heather moors. There are at least sixty-seven species of upland breeding birds, a quarter of which can be considered rare or at risk, and sixty-one are associated either with Calluna Heaths, grassy moors or acid bogs. There is probably a greater mixture of bird species typical of different climatic zones breeding in the British uplands than in any other comparably sized part of Europe.*

All is not quite lost. In fact, provided that our human intervention in these places is not simply to erect more and more fencing, or to dig deep ditches into the peat, we have little reason to hesitate before getting involved with the natural world, or what of it has come down to us. Entirely natural ecosystems are not, inevitably, the most productive, the richest in biodiversity. Asked what they believe to be the richest ecosystem on earth, many people would unhesitatingly opt for the tropical rainforest of the Amazon Basin, and would use words, such as 'diverse and natural' to describe it. In this they would be wrong, as the fairly young forests of the Amazon are not entirely natural, untouched and unworked by human hand. Far from it. The great richness of life found there has been subtly, but quite systematically manipulated (quite a lot of it actually 'gardened') by a significant population that worked with, and within the constraints of, the natural world around them. And, in so doing, made it richer. That is the wisdom we need to rediscover, and to practise.

In all this, we have an understandable tendency to look at big things, some much bigger than others: Paul Lister at Alladale wants us to have moose or the wolf, John Lister-Kaye and Paul Ramsay have espoused the cause of the beaver, which is rather more to the point. And I am, as you may have gathered, rather worried about trees, which would at least feed the beavers. But I believe that to continue to keep the planet habitable for our ungrateful and careless species, and all the creatures of delight with which we share it, we must look at things much smaller and infinitely less glamorous. At occasional intervals, I try to read two small books, and to understand them, which I do with difficulty as I am no scientist. They are both by James Lovelock: *Gaia: A New look at Life on Earth* (Oxford University Press, revised edition, 1995), and *The Revenge of Gaia* (Allen Lane, 2006). In the latter, one short sentence stays in my mind: 'My friend and collaborator Lynn Margulis more than anyone has stressed the primary importance of micro-organisms in Gaia.' What I think this means is that it is the tiny, slimy things that hold it all together, which actually keep it going, the lichens and the slime-moulds, the oozes and strange deposits. As an adult, it is so easy to ignore them completely, to stop wondering why they exist and what they actually do.

When I was a child, however, I happily played among them, down at their level, felt their slipperiness in my hands. Yes, it was, of course, in Glenleraig, down on the tidal flats from where I photographed our cottage. This was a complicated area of dissected saltings, in whose narrow channels my brother and I searched with our nets for the tiny shrimp- and prawn-like creatures, the baby flounders, the wriggling elvers and the three-spined sticklebacks. We sank into a small world of minute, semi-transparent creatures, collected bits of squidgy weed, walked on the short, glutinous turf. We did not understand why or how it all fitted together, and I could not tell you now how I think it works, but we accepted it and revelled in it. The world was very beautiful then; we must tread very gently, and keep it so.

Appendix I

THE PROBLEM OF THE DEER

The spectacular increase both in the number of red deer, and in their range, is one of the most fundamental of the environmental problems facing the Highlands. While the question still seems to be controversial in some quarters, it is at least a fairly tangible problem and one that we ought to be able to get to grips with. Whether or not the actual numbers matter enormously is not so clear to me, but where the deer now are most certainly does. As far as I can tell, the example of the red deer in Assynt may be indicative of their progress in many parts of our area.

When I was young, walking the Assynt hinterland some fifty years ago, red deer were rarely seen, and if we did actually see a stag, my father solemnly recorded it in his diary. As I have mentioned, there was a small, shy group of hinds (with one or two stags) that actually lived in the woods and emerged in the evening to browse the heather of the 'Hanging Valley' of Glenleraig. I imagine that their shyness was the result of regular local poaching, which also kept their numbers fairly constant. The birch wood was at that time clearly regenerating along its edges, but perhaps more so down by the shore and close to the houses, where the deer very rarely, if ever, appeared. We almost never saw any in the lovely meadow of the Back Park, for instance (this may have been partly because nearly all houses had dogs).

By the time I returned to live in the glen, in the 1990s, the deer on the Assynt hinterland were so numerous that, from the ridge of Quinag, you could easily trace several tracks that they made in regular movements across the whole 'plateau'. It does not often seem to be recorded that when deer move into a 'new' area in this way they behave in a very different fashion from that known and well-documented in traditional forests. For a start the hinds are not hefted, and at times you may in fact have small family groups – a stag, a few hinds and calves – roaming together: I have seen this behaviour several times in Sleat. But often they will gather in larger groups, again with both sexes and all ages. These groups are highly mobile and in the Assynt hinterland could easily be on the plateau above the head of Glenleraig one day, and up the Clachtoll Peat Road the next. This is a distance of several miles, but nothing to a deer and, on this plateau, the movement around the landscape seems to replace the vertical movement (up and down the hills during a full 24 hours) within the traditional forest. They will also regularly move into the woods at any time of the year. (This high mobility may mean, of course, that one proprietor, on an occasional count, may decide that 'this year' they have no deer, and that culling must be drastically cut back).

Although the larger herds may exhibit the normal, some-what nervous behaviour of deer, smaller groups and individuals most noticeably do not always do so, and may seem calm and relaxed in the presence of humans at all times other than during the stalking season. I regularly had to shoo stags and hinds away from close to the cottage, especially when I was parking the car, and opening the front door of the cottage only caused them to look up. I can only interpret this as the confident behaviour of animals that are no longer poached at all. On or near roads, this behaviour has been most marked for many years, and the lack of fear of cars is certainly leading to occasional but nasty accidents, and many 'near misses'. In general, proprietors seem to be content to do nothing about this at all, an attitude that is not always appreciated by local residents.

The question of 'ownership' of wild deer is one where the advantage has always seemed to be with the proprietor. As is generally known (I assume), the estates do not own the deer, which are wild animals, but own the right to shoot them. An intelligently run estate will always act promptly if there are complaints of marauding deer, and try to deal with the offending creature, but this is, obviously, always after the event, after the damage is done. And not all estates bother, or succeed, in solving the problem. Now that there are deer at any time of year throughout the dense and extensive woods of coastal Assynt, it is very difficult to predict where they will turn up next, and keeping them out of anywhere is almost impossible. I was always surprised how meekly most of us accepted that, if we wanted to grow anything at all, we would have to surround it with a deer fence – and pay for it. It is true, of course, that if a deer is eating everything in your garden, you appear to have the right to shoot it, but even in the country, not everyone has a permit, a rifle or the ability or desire to deal with a newly-shot stag. It is under circumstances like this that it may be felt that some proprietors try to have all the advantages of possessing the right to shoot, but admit to few, if any, responsibilities for the creatures they, and only they, may cull.

Even proprietors of relatively small areas of ground can also cause problems for their neighbours if they refuse to cull, when they declare the ground that they own as 'sanctuary'. This means that a small, discrete patch of ground may be the base from which quite a number of deer sally out and graze constantly on a neighbour's field or in the woods, fleeing back to their sanctuary at the first sign of trouble. The number of deer that a proprietor can have on their land should most certainly be limited to those which the land, and that land alone, could support in the long term. All this is made far more problematic by the very genuine difficulties of counting highly mobile groups under such conditions (especially in the woodland), let alone actually culling them. The compartmentalised nature of our modern Highlands, and the impossibility of growing anything without fences, adds significantly to the overall problem, as all fences (many of which are very poorly constructed, in any case) become 'porous' very rapidly, something that the deer almost seem to know.

Because of the inherent difficulty of so doing – and no doubt because of the presence of houses, domestic animals, and so on – few proprietors yet seem to do anything about culling deer within these woods, and, judging by the condition of some of them, there are now deer that simply never venture out on to the open hill, but happily spend their lives in and around the woods. They are, therefore, not culled, generally well-fed and presumably have a high breeding rate. What is clear, of course, is that they may still be very hungry after a long bad winter, and it is at this stage they will eat everything and anything; I have seen them munching on rushes, rhododendron and Japanese knot-weed (whether it does them any good or not, I have no idea, but they certainly came back for more). This is when the tender young regenerating birch, or even alder, is absolutely hammered, and this is what we must prevent if we want these woods to continue to exist into the future.

This whole problem needs to be given serious attention by the relevant bodies, and solutions looked for. We simply cannot try to fence all the areas around existing woods where regeneration should take place. Imaginative solutions are possible: in Namibia, for example, through the valuable work of the Cheetah Conservation Fund, local flocks of goats are protected against marauding cheetahs by vociferous herd dogs (from Turkey), reared for the purpose. *BBC Wildlife* (Summer 2013) reports that 'Italian "Maremma" sheepdogs have saved a penguin colony [from foxes] off the coast of Australia' in the same way. We have to be prepared to think long and hard, and laterally, to solve the problem caused by this highly contentious part of the Victorian legacy. The responsibilities of those who hold shooting rights need to be widened and strengthened; they too must play their part.

These woods are crucial to the landscape of the Scottish Highlands and Islands at so many levels, from the global to the local. They are important bastions of biodiversity in a region where that precious quality is significantly diminishing. They cannot simply be allowed to fade out, having survived through so many difficulties up to now.

At the other end of the deer range, on the high moors where there are existing peat-hags, black and wearisome to cross, it is again crucial that trampling does not further erode the exposed peat, causing it to oxidise, releasing carbon dioxide. I know some deer forests where each hag is cut up by the passage of countless sharp hooves, and their edges pushed back each year, widening the eroding area. This must stop, and just as with the woods, the relevant parties need to work together to look for solutions, which have to be found. I admit this will not be easy, and there will be those who will resist even thinking about it, but ownership of land carries with it, implicitly, as many responsibilities as it does privileges, and it is high time these were made explicit.

This problem of deer numbers and behaviour was long in the making, and it will clearly not be solved quickly, but we have to try. Any idea of a 'natural population' of red deer in the Scottish Highlands is both irrelevant and impossible to define. For centuries, perhaps even for thousands of years, the surprisingly widely distributed human population, dependent on agriculture for food (with, presumably, some venison for high days and holidays), kept the population of deer limited both in numbers and in range. Up until the 1700s, wolves must have assisted in that process. The Victorians took a very different view and encouraged numbers to increase significantly, a process which seems to have become unstoppable in recent decades. Things cannot go on like this and estates must play their part in working out how best to limit effectively both range and numbers. Although I hope that other measures will be devised and used, culling, probably on an increased scale, will be needed into the indefinite future, gamekeepers will be guaranteed jobs, and the predictable hysterical cries that it will all mean the end of the sporting estate will be absolute nonsense.

Appendix II

TREES OF THE HIGHLAND ARBORETUMS

I did not fully appreciate the considerable diversity of species of the many arboretums of the Highlands and Islands until I was working at Aigas Field Centre. It was then that I first met John Miller of Alness, whose little book *Trees of the Northern Highlands* (Inver Ross Printing Co. Ltd., 1999) is the modest product of much time, patience and enormous enthusiasm. To illustrate the richness of this botanical legacy of the Victorian era, I have simply listed below the more common species found in a number of locations by this quietly remarkable man.

The first group below lists particularly fine specimens to be found at Aigas:

Nikko Fir
Lawson Cypress
Nootka Cypress
Norway Spruce
Caucasian Spruce
Giant Sequoia
Eastern Hemlock
Sycamore Variegatum
Red Oak
Cut-leaf Lime

In addition, the following are widely found:

Silver Fir
Grand Fir
Caucasian Fir
Noble Fir
Monkey Puzzle
Atlas Cedar
Himalayan Cedar
Cedar of Lebanon
Leyland Cypress
European Larch
(True) Cypress
Dawn Redwood
Sitka Spruce
Lodgepole Pine
Beech
Copper Beech
Common Walnut
Prickly Castor-Oil Tree
Tulip Tree
London Plane

Grey Poplar
Black Poplar
Turkey Oak
Holm Oak

Appendix III

AIGAS FIELD CENTRE

The House of Aigas is beautifully situated on the north side of the lower valley of the River Beauly, just above the point where its waters divide around the romantic, tree-girt isle of Eileanaigas before entering the deep gorge. The main house was built in 1877 by a family of Glasgow merchants, the Gordon-Oswalds, and this Victorian edifice conceals an earlier, more modest Fraser house of around 1760. Like so many others, it became the centre of a Victorian sporting estate, complete with arboretum, gardens, Home Farm and estate village, with plantations and an enlarged loch nestling below the sweep of moorland, where, annually, red grouse were sought-out and shot.

In the 1950s, the house was purchased by the Inverness County Council to function as an old folks' home. It was endowed with the depressing name of 'The Aigas Terminal Home' and its fine rooms were converted to institutional use, with the large bedrooms becoming wards and, inevitably, the elaborate grounds being neglected. This period of decline lasted until 1971 when it was simply abandoned to the elements; the one good thing about this final event was that its roof was not removed, as happened to so many other large, redundant buildings of this type.

So it remained, unloved and unwanted, until John Lister-Kaye realised its potential as the base for the successor to the Highland Wildlife Enterprises business that he had established further up Strath Glass. Aigas was to become, as it has remained since, very much a dual-purpose creation: both a comfortable family home and the base for the first residential Field Centre to be established in the Highlands. For the latter purpose, the big public rooms including the baronial hall were opened to public use, while overnight accommodation was provided in new timber lodges in the wooded grounds. The immediate surroundings provided plenty of scope for observation and study, but it was also an ideal base from which to explore the wide range of interest and delight that characterise the Highlands and Islands. Slowly, over the years, the idea has matured and grown, the Field Centre and its activities have developed and expanded, winning many friends worldwide, while patient hours have greatly enhanced the natural beauty of its setting.

From early on, there were two sides to the activities of the Field Centre: while it provides wildlife holidays and study programmes to adults, its charitable arm, the Aigas Trust for Environmental Education, raises funds to provide environmental education to around 6,000 schoolchildren and young adults every year. For many years, while guests have been out looking for eagles in neighbouring glens, enthusiastic groups of children have been exploring the natural world in the woods around the house, work that has been greatly facilitated by the construction of the impressive purpose-built space of The Magnus House, opened in 2009 by HRH Prince Charles, Duke of Rothesay.

Aigas, now managed by John's son, Warwick, celebrates its 39th season in 2016. In the beautifully illustrated programme for 2015, John Lister-Kaye's welcoming letter referred to the fact that the year before was the centenary of the birth of Gavin

Maxwell, author of *Ring of Bright Water*. John worked with him towards the end of his life in 1969, and it was from that short but crucial experience that the idea of Aigas evolved. I have already shown how Gavin Maxwell was, in his youth, passionately devoted to the cult of the sporting estate, an ethos that would have exterminated, without a moment's hesitation, the very otters he wrote about, and which helped make his name and attracted so many people to the Highlands and Islands of Scotland. Similarly, Aigas has evolved, under the guidance of John Lister-Kaye, from a typical Victorian sporting estate (where the supremacy of man over nature was unquestioned) into a place where the joy of the natural world, and its ability to sustain and enhance our lives, may be experienced by all.

Appendix IV

THE REALITY OF HIGHLAND POPULATION FIGURES

I have made several references to Professor Chris Smout in this book and he kindly read through a draft, and made a number of points. Perhaps the most significant of these concerned the population statistics that are available for the Highlands and Islands during the Victorian period. As *Castles in the Mist* is not a treatise on movements in the Highland population, and because I am far from sure that I understand the full implications of these figures, it seemed best to me to deal briefly with the subject in this appendix. It is fair, I think, to say that many will find some of the figures surprising – I certainly did – and very much at odds with the conventional wisdom on the period.

I have tried to ensure that my foregoing text is not too much at variance with the reality represented by these figures, a task that would be easier if I understood exactly what they mean. The information below is that supplied by Chris Smout.

Personally, I think you might need to talk much more about population. For example, the population of Sutherland was estimated by Webster at 20,774 in 1755, but censused in 1801 at 23,117, rising (despite the Sutherland Clearances) in 1831 to 25,518 – this is a considerable rise in a poor county. The most likely explanation is that potato husbandry allowed more people to subsist from the same extent of ground [although in Assynt, around 1800, a number of sheilings appear to have been taken over for permanent occupation – Robin Noble], and probably they chose to marry younger. Of course the Clearances redistributed population to the coast [although, again in Assynt, that coast was already regarded as congested by 1775 – Robin Noble]. Population was down by about 650 by 1841, but despite the famine rose to 25,793 in 1851 – this was Sutherland's all-time high; you would have expected it to fall during the famine but the Duke was very generous to the starving.

By the 1860s clearances were starting to become less acceptable and in the 1880s the crofters got security of tenure, but population by 1911 was down to 20,179, the first time it fell below the 1755 baseline peak. Then came a sharp drop (at a time of total legal protection against eviction) to 13,664 in 1951.

The period with the sharp reduction from 1911 to 1951 did obviously include the two World Wars and it seems entirely fair to deduce that at least a significant part of that steep fall was due to the different but cumulative effect of the two conflicts (which were, of course, only twenty years apart), to which I referred in the main text. Chris Smout continues:

Perhaps the best account of Highland population history is in Chapter Three of Fraser Darling's West Highland Survey (Oxford University Press, 1955), the tables of which are particularly worthy of close study. In that study area, the peak of population is reached in 1831, with 1841 virtually the same, and the steepest decline came in the 1850s and 1920s, the latter being the maximum. Population here was higher in 1901 than in 1801, and higher in 1951 than in 1755.

He concludes: 'Population is the elephant in the room for Clearance studies', having, I think, demonstrated precisely that!

The difference in the 1951 figures for the West Highland Survey area, and for Sutherland – one being higher than the figure for 1755, and the other much lower – make it clear to me that this is an area of study where generalisations are almost meaningless. A great deal of detailed work would need to be undertaken before a proper understanding of these changes could be reached. That lies far beyond the scope of this book. None of this is to deny the reality of the Clearances, of emigration, or the effect of the two World Wars, or the results we see in the countryside, the abandoned farms, or the empty glens. Where, it seems, we may still be missing something, is in understanding all the different factors that led to growth in the Highland population during this complex period.

REFERENCES

This section contains publications that have been referred to explicitly in the main text AND publications that have been used as sources of background information.

Beaton, Elizabeth, *Sutherland: An Illustrated Architectural Guide*, Royal Incorporation of Architects in Scotland/Landmark Trust, 1995. Courtesy of Neil Baxter at RIAS

Beaton, Elizabeth, *Ross and Cromarty: An Illustrated Architectural Guide*, Royal Incorporation of Architects in Scotland/Landmark Trust, 1992. Courtesy of Neil Baxter at RIAS

Burgher, Leslie, *Orkney: An Illustrated Architectural Guide*, Royal Incorporation of Architects in Scotland/Landmark Trust, 1991. Courtesy of Neil Baxter at RIAS

Dodgshon, Robert, *The Age of the Clans*, Historic Scotland/Birlinn, 2002. Courtesy of Peter Burns at Birlinn

Gunn, Neil M., *Highland River*, The Porpoise Press, 1937. Also published by Canongate, 1997

Harrison, E.P., *Scottish Estate Tweeds*, Johnstons of Elgin, 1995

Linklater, Eric, *Orkney and Shetland*, Robert Hale, 1965

Lister-Kaye, Sir John, Bt., 'Ill Fares the Land: A Sustainable Land Ethic for the Sporting Estates of the Highlands and Islands of Scotland', Scottish Natural Heritage, Occasional Paper Number 3, 1994. Extracts reproduced by kind permission of SNH and Sir John Lister-Kaye

Lovelock, James, *Gaia*, Oxford University Press, revised edition, 1995

Lovelock, James, *The Revenge of Gaia*, Allen Lane, 2006

Mabey, Richard, 'A Brush with Nature', *BBC Wildlife*, March 2014. Courtesy of Matt Swaine at *BBC Wildlife*

Mabey, Richard, *The Ash and the Beech: The Drama of Woodland Changes*, Vintage, 2007. © Richard Mabey, 2007. Extracts reproduced by kind permission of Sheil Land Associates Ltd.

Macdonald, Claire, *Claire Macdonald's Scotland: The Best of Scottish Food and Drink*, Little, Brown & Co., 1990

Mackenzie, Compton, *The Monarch of the Glen*, Penguin, 1941. Also published by Vintage, 2009

Magnusson, Magnus, *Rum: Nature's Island*, Luath Press Ltd., 1997

Maxwell, Gavin, *Ring of Bright Water*, Longmans, 1960. Also published by Little Toller, 2014. Extract reproduced by kind permission of Little Toller

McKean, Charles, *Moray: An Illustrated Architectural Guide*, Royal Incorporation of Architects in Scotland/Landmark Trust, 1987. Courtesy of Neil Baxter at RIAS

Miller, John, *Trees of the Northern Highlands*, Inver Ross Printing Co., 1999

Monbiot, George, 'Why the Grass Isn't Greener', *BBC Wildlife*, Summer 2013. Courtesy of Matt Swaine at *BBC Wildlife*

Munro of Foulis, Hector, *Foulis Castle*, Jarrold Publishing, 2013. Courtesy of Hector Munro

Nicolaisen, W.F.H, *Scottish Place-names*, Batsford, 1976

Noble, Robin, *North and West*, Scottish Cultural Press, 2003

Pearsall, W.H., *Mountains and Moorlands*, Fontana New Naturalist Series, 1968

Ramsay, Paul, *Revival of the Land: Creag Meagaidh National Nature Reserve*, Scottish Natural Heritage, 1997. Extracts reproduced by kind permission of SNH

Roberts, Neil, *The Holocene: An Environmental History*, Wiley-Blackwell, 1998. Extract reproduced by kind permission of Wiley

Scott, Alastair, *Eccentric Wealth: The Bulloughs of Rum*, Birlinn, 2011

Scottish History Society, *John Home's Survey of Assynt*, Edinburgh, 1960. Extract reproduced by kind permission of SHS

Scottish Natural Heritage, *Scotland's Wild Deer: A National Approach*, 2015

Scottish Natural Heritage with Royal Commission on the Ancient and Historical Monuments of Scotland, *RUM: Kinloch Castle*, 1999

Smith, Alexander, *A Summer in Skye*, 1865. Also published by Birlinn, 1998

Smout, T.C., *Nature Contested*, Edinburgh University Press, 2000. Extracts reproduced by kind permission of T.C. Smout and EUP

Smout, T.C., *Scotland since Prehistory: Natural Change and Human Impact*, Scottish Cultural Press, 1993.

Smout, T.C., 'The Highlands and the Roots of Green Consciousness, 1750–1990', Scottish Natural Heritage, Occasional Paper Number 1, 1993. Originally published in *Proceedings of the British Academy*, Volume 76. © The British Academy, 1991. Extracts reproduced by kind permission of the British Academy.

Strathnaver, Lord, *Dunrobin Castle*, Heritage House Group Ltd., 2003

Thomson, William P.L., *New History of Orkney*, Mercat Press/Birlinn, 1987. Extract reproduced by kind permission of Birlinn

Walsh, Maurice, *The Key above the Door*, Chambers, 1926. Also published by Balnain Books, 1991

The author also made use of various publications produced by Historic Assynt, including: *Historic Assynt Magazine*, No. 3, 2012; *Calda House and the MacKenzies of Assynt*, 2008; *Castles, Clans and Churches*, 2007. Courtesy of Historic Assynt

ACKNOWLEDGEMENTS

Anyone who tries to get a book published is grateful for efficiency and courtesy; in recent years I think particularly of Moira Forsyth of Sandstone Press, Lucy Duckworth of Unicorn Press, Shirley Greenall of Whittet Books, and Jenny Brown, the literary agent who suggested I should contact Sara Hunt. Encouraged by these responses, I did exactly that and serendipitously, subsequently met Sara at Aigas, where we and others were enjoying the fabulous hospitality of John and Lucy Lister-Kaye. This brief history led directly to the writing of this book, and I am grateful to all of them for the helpful part they played.

Once you get into the writing of a book, it is easy to end up too close to it, knowing the text off by heart, and external comment is vital. I am particularly grateful to those other writers who have given most generously of their time to go through my text and make valuable comments; I refer to John Lister-Kaye, Chris Smout and Lesley McLaren. Friends and relations have helped, especially Andy Bluefield, Rhoderick Noble, Mary Stow and Martine Howard. The wonders of modern technology occasionally drive me frantic, but have meant that Kirsty MacLeod has kept the whole edifice in order, while also adding her own helpful comments.

I am of course most grateful to the whole team at Saraband; especially to Sara Hunt for her belief in this book, to Craig Hillsley who has made the editing process much more pleasant than I had expected, and to Hannah Fields for editorial assistance. I am also most grateful to Sir John Lister-Kaye for writing a foreword; working at Aigas has obviously been a major stimulus to much of the thinking behind this book.

My thanks are due, too, to the great number of folk with whom I have explored the Highlands and Islands over the decades, and discussed almost everything under the sun (and the clouds and in the midges). The stimulus of their questions has helped me organise my thoughts, a crucial part of the whole process. And among those, I must mention all the countless Rangers at Aigas Field Centre, who for so long have been handed over to me for a week during their annual intensive training; what they really think of it, I dare not imagine, but it has always been the best job I have ever had – despite the vagaries of the weather!

INDEX